Th Religious Trauma Survival Guide

Education + Recovery Tools

Anna Clark Miller

First Edition: September 2023

Second Edition: April 2024

Edited by Carl Miller

ISBN: 979-8-9891048-0-2 (ebook)

ISBN: 979-8-9891048-1-9 (paperback)

Published by Empathy Paradigm

Table of Contents

Introduction

Recovering from religious trauma requires a significant amount of time, effort, and emotional energy and none of us should have to navigate it with unnecessary barriers. This book aims to provide clear, unbiased information and practical tools to make the healing process more accessible. Transparency about the perspective I'm writing from is crucial to set the tone.

As a survivor of religious trauma, I understand the anxiety that arises from perceived hidden agendas, particularly those tied to religion. In my experience, information on religious trauma recovery is most effective when communicated from a religiously neutral standpoint. This allows you the freedom to focus on your healing journey without fear that a religious bias is being pushed on you.

For those reasons, I've tried to maintain a balanced view, neither advocating for nor against any religious stance in this book. I have no interest in swaying your spiritual beliefs or religious affiliation. I do, however, want to be transparent about my personal spiritual journey and how that might influence my perspectives in this book.

After over 35 years as an Evangelical Christian, I stopped attending church in 2019. Currently, I don't align myself with any religious group, largely due to my experiences of religious trauma. At its core, I just don't feel safe in organized religious settings. This choice is not a critique of religion itself, though. I celebrate those who find fulfillment in their faith and I'm open to one day exploring that aspect of my life again.

In this book, I'll present educational content on religious trauma and patterns of religious abuse, but I'll steer clear of debating the merits or drawbacks of religion. As you read, you will probably encounter content that challenges your personal beliefs or views. That's okay! As a reader and autonomous individual, you're free to form your own interpretations and make your own choices.

What to Expect

Encountering emotional discomfort, confusion, or intrusive thoughts when confronting trauma and abuse is entirely normal. Rather than allowing that to make you feel trapped or hopeless, try to acknowledge those reactions, validate your feelings, and practice self-compassion.

Contrary to what you may have been taught in the past, it's your right (and responsibility) to care for your own mental and physical well-being. You may find it helpful to periodically check in with yourself to gauge how you're coping, engage in self-care, and make adjustments. There's no rush—give yourself permission to move through this process at your pace, listening to what your body and emotions are telling you, and investing however much time and energy you find beneficial.

During recovery, it's common to grapple with self-judgment and a tendency to moralize (often evident in thoughts framed around concepts of "right," "wrong," "good," or "bad.") Remember, your journey through religious trauma recovery is not an exam; it's a path toward healing without any grading system. If perfectionism surfaces, resist the impulse to criticize yourself. Instead, lean into curiosity and openness to new insights.

This book is structured into two distinct parts to guide your journey towards healing. **Part One** aims to educate you about religious trauma: its definition, origins, and how it presents itself, and **Part Two** of the book will focus on practical recovery tools for you to put into practice. Both parts will include periodic reflection questions and self-inventories to assist with integrating the content with your personal experiences.

Rather than viewing the reflection prompts and inventories in this book as assessments of your recovery progress, think of them as opportunities to explore your inner landscape so you can decide where you want to go next. Should you feel overwhelmed at any point, remember it's perfectly okay to take breaks, seek support, or pause your journey while you find a therapist to process it with.

An Important Disclaimer

This book is not a substitute for professional therapy. It's designed to be a supplementary resource, recognizing that some experiences of religious trauma are too complex to be fully addressed here. If you experience thoughts of self-harm, severe anxiety, panic, dissociation, flashbacks, or PTSD symptoms, immediate professional support is advised. A list of resources for accessing trauma-informed therapy is provided at the book's conclusion.

A Note on Language Diversity

Efforts were made to ensure the inclusivity of the language used in this book, though some terms might resonate more with individuals from American evangelical backgrounds. Readers from different religious traditions might find it necessary to mentally substitute certain terms to reflect their experiences more accurately.

PART ONE: EDUCATION

Our journey begins with differentiating **spirituality** from **religion**, a distinction that will be important throughout the healing process.

Spirituality refers to a deeply personal connection to something larger than oneself. This connection might be with God, nature, other people, ideas, or any entity that holds deep significance. The beauty of spirituality lies in its individuality—no one has the authority to declare another's spiritual journey as correct or incorrect.

> At its core, spirituality is "a subjective experience of the sacred."[1]

Religion, in contrast, refers to a spiritual community's collective aspects: their ideology, doctrine, policies, rituals, and practices. These structures identify a religious group, but they don't represent each members' subjective experience. While spirituality and religion often intertwine, engaging in religious practices doesn't guarantee a spiritual experience and finding spiritual connection doesn't exclusively happen in religious settings.

---

1 Vaughan, F. (1991) Spiritual Issues in Psychotherapy.

Chapter 1: Understanding Religious Trauma

Our bodies are constantly communicating to us through physical and emotional signals that are crucial for navigating life effectively. They communicate everything from basic needs like hunger to complex emotions like fear, anger, or hurt. Our survival hinges on our ability to hear, interpret, and respond to these signals, especially when facing danger.

Threat Responses

When threatened, our nervous system kicks into gear without needing conscious input from us, automatically deploying survival strategies known as the "Fight-or-Flight" responses. Research has expanded our understanding of threat responses to include these four primary types: Fight, Flight, Freeze, and Fawn.

The **four threat responses** play a critical role in our survival, each enabling us to navigate threatening situations by instinct.

A Fight Response deals with threats head-on by prompting us to attack before we are attacked. While a physical altercation is the most obvious example, this also includes non-physical forms of confrontation. Some examples of non-violent fight responses are verbal arguing, criticizing, mocking, posturing, and making threats.

A Flight Response helps us escape from the danger as quickly as possible by fleeing or avoiding it.

These can manifest through any physical or mental behavior that's aimed at evading or avoiding confrontation. Some examples of mental flight responses include distracting ourselves with busy work, numbing ourselves with substances, refusing to stop and rest, and procrastinating.

A Freeze Response is a state of immobilization that helps us escape danger by being inconspicuous and staying under the radar until the threat has passed. This can be seen in nature when animals "play dead" to convince a predator that they're not worth attacking. When our fight and flight options aren't available, can find ourselves mentally "spacing out," feeling unable to move, think, or speak until the danger seems to be gone.

A Fawn Response is a learned behavior that can buy us temporary safety through pleasing or appeasing the source of the threat. When other threat responses don't work, we'll try to placate or pacify a threatening person by being overly polite, flattering, or submissive. We might make promises, take blame, or apologize to make ourselves useful to someone who could hurt us.

As we delve deeper into the ways that spiritual and religious trauma can impact us, these threat responses are crucial to keep in mind. They allow us to empathize with the diverse paths that others take and can help us find compassion for ourselves too. Our understanding of religious trauma is grounded in respect for the complex ways that someone might try to navigate threats in a religious setting.

Reflect

Do you intentionally try to listen to what your body's telling you? How?

What are the possible consequences of not listening to your body's threat responses?

Which of the four threat responses do you gravitate toward? What are some examples?

In what situations do you notice threat responses?

Trauma

Have you experienced trauma? That can be a hard question to answer. While the term "trauma" gets thrown around a lot in current events and on social media, there's value in knowing its' clinical definition and the different types of trauma we can experience.

> At its' most basic, trauma is an experience that provokes overwhelming **terror and helplessness**.

When someone experiences trauma, their fight, flight, freeze, or fawn threat responses often get increasingly intense. People with PTSD often perceive that threats are happening all around them all the time, trapping their nervous system in a miserable cycle of triggers and threat responses.

In the wake of a traumatic event, people may notice short-term or long-term symptoms. American Psychological Association says that "immediately after the event, shock and denial are typical. Longer-term reactions include unpredictable emotions, flashbacks, strained relationships, and even physical symptoms."

Each person's response to a traumatic experience is completely unique, however. Even if two people experience the exact same adverse event, they may not have the same perspective on what happened, how harmful it was, or even whether it was traumatic or not.

When people experience lots of smaller events that make them feel unsafe, chronic trauma can occur.

This is different from acute trauma which comes from a major terrifying event that doesn't necessarily continue over time. Both of these types of trauma are legitimate.

Our responses to trauma have a lot of other contributing factors. Someone's genetics, childhood development, brain type, social support, coping skills, and access to treatment can all make a major difference. Additionally, the type, duration, and severity of the trauma itself are big factors.

PTSD

Post-Traumatic Stress Disorder (PTSD) has only been researched for the past 100 years or so. Each year we learn more about what it is, what the symptoms can look like, and what the risk factors are. Recent studies suggest that simply having a family history of trauma might increase someone's risk of PTSD.

To be formally diagnosed with PTSD, someone needs to meet the criteria listed in the Diagnostic and Statistical Manual, Version 5 (DSM-V). A Complex-PTSD diagnosis has also been added to medical manuals in recent years. Hopefully, a Religious Trauma diagnosis will eventually be added as well.

> The nervous system of someone with PTSD is in a constant state of overdrive, leaving them feeling stuck in **survival mode** long after the original threat has passed.

Not every person who experiences trauma will end up with PTSD, however. Even if someone has trauma symptoms, they may not qualify for a formal diagnosis. Before we go over the major symptoms of PTSD, let's identify what it means in general terms.

Symptoms of PTSD

An official diagnosis of PTSD would require that multiple symptoms co-occur over an extended period of time. These are some of the most common ones.

- **Hypervigilance**: A state of high tension and anxiety while compulsively monitoring your surroundings for any potential threats.

- **Exaggerated Startle Response**: Having intense physical reactions to unexpected noises, sensations, or changes in your environment.

- **Flashbacks**: An involuntary reliving of your past traumatic experience(s), often including the emotional or physical responses that were originally present.

- **Avoidance**: Repeatedly trying to reduce your exposure to reminders of the traumatic experience(s).

- **Social Withdrawal**: Social isolation or increased difficulty connecting with others.

- **Dissociation**: Mental or emotional detachment and/or disconnection from your surroundings when feeling uncomfortable or unsafe.

- **Sleep Disturbance**: Insomnia (difficulty falling or staying asleep), nightmares, or night terrors.

- **Recklessness or Self-Neglect:** Intentional or unintentional acts that put you in danger or increase risks to your physical or mental health.

- **Depression**: Feelings of hopelessness, increased irritability, excessive guilt, or shame, and low motivation to do things you previously enjoyed.

Reflect

What kinds of religious teachings or experiences might cause trauma?

Have you ever felt terrified or helpless in a religious context?

What are the risks or benefits of someone accepting that they have trauma responses?

Do you think you experience trauma responses? If so, when did they start?

Have you ever tried to ignore your trauma responses? If so, what was the outcome?

Religious Trauma

Religious trauma happens when someone is overwhelmed or harmed by a religious experience or teaching. It's marked by physical, emotional, or psychological responses that make it hard for the survivor to cope and feel safe even after the experience is over.

Adverse Religious Experiences are any "religious belief, practice, or structure that undermines an individual's sense of safety or autonomy and/or negatively impacts their physical, social, emotional, relational, or psychological well-being."[2]

Religious trauma can be acute, chronic, or complex. Acute religious trauma comes from a single traumatic experience, while chronic or complex religious trauma comes from repeated experiences that may happen over a long time. All of these types of trauma are legitimate and can be experienced in a variety of religious settings.

People sometimes refer to these experiences as "religious abuse" or "spiritual abuse" instead of trauma. But religious trauma and religious abuse are two different things and it's a distinction worth making.

The technical definition of abuse, according to the American Psychological Association is a behavior that's cruel, violent, demeaning, or invasive toward

---

2 The Religious Trauma Institute. (2019) Adverse Religious Experiences.

someone else. The same is true of abuse in a spiritual or religious setting[3].

Spiritual Abuse is "the mistreatment of a person who is in need of help, support, or greater spiritual empowerment, with the result of weakening, undermining, or decreasing that person's spiritual empowerment."[4]

Saying that someone has been abused implies there was a perpetrator who inflicted harm on them. While many people with religious trauma have experienced clear abuse from religious leaders or authorities, not every instance of religious trauma is caused by spiritual abuse.

Survivors can experience religious trauma even if there isn't a clear **perpetrator** who can be labeled as the "abuser."

Additionally, most people who harm others through traumatizing religious beliefs and practices are themselves victims of those same things. Abusive religious groups are often filled with and led by well-intentioned victims who are unwittingly repeating the cycle of abuse by passing on the same harmful beliefs and practices that have traumatized them. For those reasons, some prefer to use the term "religious trauma" because it makes fewer assumptions about

3 Ward, D. (2011) The Lived Experience of Spiritual Abuse.
4 Johnson & VanVonderen. (2005) The Subtle Power of Spiritual Abuse.

who inflicted the trauma and what their intentions were.

Regardless of which term we use, it's important not to downplay the impacts of true religious abuse. Whether religious leaders have good intentions or not, the impact of their actions is the same. When abuse happens in the context of religion or spirituality, it causes a unique wound that can be very difficult to identify, validate, and heal.

Reflect

Do you think religious trauma counts as "real" trauma? Why?

Does the term religious abuse seem harsh or unfair? Why?

If you've experienced religious trauma, do you think abuse was involved?

If one religious group member feels traumatized or abused, does that mean everyone else in the group is too? Why or why not?

Alarm Signals

Imagine that your home has a smoke alarm that's supposed to alert you if there's a fire. If the alarm goes off but you can't see any smoke or fire, you might assume it was broken. The irritating sound would make you turn it off or take out the batteries just to get some peace and quiet. While disabling the alarm might lower your momentary stress, it would leave you vulnerable if there were an actual fire you needed to know about.

When we spend a long time in a traumatizing environment, it's common for us to start tuning out or numbing our body's threat responses. Denial and exhaustion make it easier to ignore the problem than to confront it. Like the disabled smoke alarm, ignoring the signals might make it easier to cope temporarily, but it won't address the real problem.

> If we habitually **ignore** our bodies' threat responses, it gets harder and harder to tell if we're in danger.

If we're going to respond appropriately to our body's alarm signals, we have to learn how to intentionally tune in. This starts with learning the language that our body uses to communicate with us. Signs that you're not feeling safe might include noticing your shoulders tense up, your stomach lurches, your breathing getting shallow, or your pulse pounding in your ears. When you notice those alarms, instead of just tuning them out, take a minute to investigate what may have triggered them.

This can be quite difficult for those who aren't in the habit of recognizing and naming complex emotions. It's even harder if our religious groups have taught us that our bodies will try to tempt or deceive us. It takes time to undo that mental programming and start listening to our bodies instead of ignoring them. Be patient with yourself if this new skill is challenging at first.

The first step of tuning into our bodies is connecting our physical sensations with our emotional experiences. Each time we practice connecting the dots between our physical and emotional experiences, we get a little bit better at recognizing the patterns. Once we've learned to interpret what our bodies are telling us, we are empowered to act. We can then get better at recognizing danger, protecting ourselves, and figuring out what true safety feels like.

"Bodies of child abuse victims are tense and defensive until they find a way to relax and feel safe. To change, people need to become aware of their sensations and the way that their bodies interact with the world around them. Physical self-awareness is the first step in releasing the tyranny of the past."[5]

5 Van der Kolk, B. (2014) The Body Keeps the Score.

Reflect

What alarm signals (body sensations or emotions) have you noticed when you've been in religious settings?

What feelings are coming up now as you think about your past religious experiences?

Do you feel any need to defend the religious group or leaders that may have harmed you? If so, why?

Does labeling your religious experience as "trauma" seem scary or invalid? If so, why?

Chapter 2: Symptoms of Religious Trauma

Authors, philosophers, and clergy members have been trying to understand the phenomenon of religious trauma for centuries but there's still not a formal diagnosis for it. Many in the psychology field have made attempts at describing and measuring its symptoms such as Marlene Winell's Religious Trauma Syndrome (RTS)[6]. Although we have these helpful frameworks, a lot of research is still needed.

In this chapter I'll share my own list of symptoms of religious trauma. The main categories are fear and anxiety, shame, rigidity and suppression, and relationship dysfunction. Each of these categories will include some of the most common expressions of that symptom and some practical examples of each.

Keep in mind, not every religious trauma survivor experiences all these symptoms. Try to read with a mindset of curiosity. If strong feelings of anger, grief, or anxiety come up, just take note of them. There's no need to silence or avoid them. Note: I refer to "high control" groups frequently in this chapter and will define that in detail in Chapter 3.

---

6 Winell, M. (2011) Religious Trauma Syndrome.

Fear + Anxiety

Most religious trauma survivors experience chronic anxiety symptoms that usually stem from fear-inducing religious teachings about practical or spiritual threats (i.e. exclusion from the group, hell, or spiritual warfare.) Some religious groups use these fear tactics to enforce control and conformity within the group or to recruit new members who are looking for safety.

Common forms of religious trauma fear and anxiety:

- **Generalized Anxiety:** Recurring worries, intrusive thoughts, difficulty relaxing or feeling safe (especially in spiritual settings); may also include panic attacks, nightmares, and phobias.

- **Afterlife Anxiety**: Fear about death, heaven and/or hell, the rapture, eternal separation from loved ones, and obsessive worries about witnessing or ensuring salvation.

- **Fear of Evil**: Intense dread or paranoia about spiritual threats like sin, temptation, demonic possession, spiritual warfare, and secular influences.

- **Scrupulosity**: Obsessive rule-following, fear of punishment or being falsely accused of wrongdoing, and paranoia about determining right from wrong.

- **Superstitions** (Compulsions): Magical thinking and/or compulsions to use religious rituals to prevent bad things from happening (OCD).

Practical Examples:

When James was ten years old, a priest told him that no one can know for sure if they'll get into paradise until they die and face God's judgment. As a teen, he has regular panic attacks about going to hell and prays every night that he'll be spared.

Nigel does his quiet time in the same way every single morning. If he misses a day or forgets a step in the process, he feels extremely anxious and dysregulated. He worries that if he messes up, he'll totally lose control.

Lisa often sees spiritual "signs" that she believes are from God. When she sees a bad sign, she is terrified that it means she's being targeted by evil spirits. She sometimes gets so anxious that she can't leave the house.

Brendan gets panicked and upset when his elderly mother talks about what she's learning at her new non-denominational church. He's terrified that she'll be brainwashed and exploited by people who don't believe the "right" things.

Reflect

What things did your religious group teach you to be afraid of?

What behaviors did your religious group say would prevent bad things from happening to you?

Have you ever been diagnosed with an anxiety disorder? If so, do you think any religious teachings have contributed?

Do you have any ritualistic or superstitious behaviors? Do they seem to be driven by anxiety?

What self-talk could you use in moments of high anxiety that might help you de-escalate?

Shame

Religious trauma survivors often place low value on their personal health and happiness. Negative self-beliefs and inability to achieve perfection often lead to a sense of inadequacy and self-hatred as well as burnout, exhaustion, and self-sabotage.

This religious trauma symptom is especially common in groups that teach that humans are fundamentally evil, sinful, or worthless on their own. Some groups even discourage healthy self-worth by labeling it "pride" or warning their members not to indulge in outside sources of comfort. This can give members the impression that suffering and self-hatred are not only normal, but ideal.

Common forms of religious trauma shame:

- **Low Self-Worth:** Negative beliefs that we're bad, broken, inadequate, insignificant, "sinful", etc.

- **Helplessness:** A sense of powerlessness or defeat, low motivation, and cynicism about the future.

- **Perfectionism:** Trying to compensate for our perceived inadequacy by overworking; using harsh self-criticism to stay focused on achievement.

- **Self-Distrust:** Lack of confidence in our own instincts and desires, self-doubt, self-sabotage, and overreliance on others.

- **Self-Neglect:** Poor self-care, unaddressed physical and mental health issues, and compulsively serving others rather than tending to personal needs.

Practical Examples:

Maria feels worthless for never living up to her own spiritual expectations. Even though others see her as wise, disciplined, and compassionate, she can't acknowledge anything positive about herself without feeling prideful.

Lori volunteers and serves in her religious group without resting or taking breaks until her body literally forces her to stop. When she's sick from exhaustion, all she can think about is how lazy and unproductive she's being.

John is married but he feels trapped by his secret habit of looking at pornography and masturbating. He can't bear the thought of talking to his wife about it because he feels like it proves he's dirty, perverted, and a sex addict.

June dreams of starting his own business but whenever he tries to make plans, he quickly spirals into self-doubt. He gives in to a premature sense of defeat, believing that it must just not be the Lord's plan for his life.

Reflect

Do you think you struggle with shame? If so, how does it impact your daily life?

What did your religious group teach you about things like self-care and your mental health?

How do you talk to yourself internally when you make a mistake? What does that tell you?

Do you ever feel incapable of making changes to improve your situation? If so, do you have any self-defeating behaviors that get your way?

Rigidity + Suppression

Many religious trauma survivors become rigid in how they think, feel, and function after long term adherence to high-control beliefs and expectations. This makes it hard for us to listen to other perspectives, be curious, or change our minds when we learn new information. Additionally, many survivors experience a wide range of symptoms that come from long-term suppression of their natural instincts, feelings, and identities.

Common forms of religious trauma rigidity and suppression:

- **Black & White Thinking:** Moralistic or binary thinking (drawing a clear line between "good and bad" or "right and wrong"), rejecting nuances and fearing compromise.

- **Poor Critical Thinking:** Impaired decision-making as a result of suppressing our curiosity, clinging to existing biases or opinions, and rejecting contradictory evidence.

- **Emotional Suppression:** Habitually invalidating or denying unaccepted emotions like anger and sadness leading to depression, avoidance, numbness, and stunted empathy.

- **Identity Suppression:** Denying or trying to change personal traits that we view as "deviant", poor self-awareness, depression, and suicidal ideation.

- **Sexual Suppression:** Emphasizing sexual conformity and purity, feeling intense guilt or shame about sex, denying sexual attractions, stunted sexual development, and inability to enjoy sex.

- **Suppression of Autonomy:** Difficulty identifying our needs and wants, lack of independence, and enmeshment (trouble separating our own thoughts and feelings from others').

- **Spiritual Cynicism:** Distrust of most (or all) spiritual and religious practices, leaders, or teachings.

- **Somatic Symptoms:** Suppressed feelings and needs that are converted into physical pain or illness (ex. fibromyalgia, headaches, high blood pressure, pain during sex, etc.)

Practical Examples:

David was taught that climate change is false because it contradicts his beliefs. When his friends try to show him scientific evidence for climate change, he gets angry and defensive and stops hanging out with them.

Nadia believes that forgiveness is always the right thing no matter what. She keeps giving her abusive husband more chances because her community has told her it would be wrong to stay separated from him.

Beatrice is adjusting to her best friend coming out as gay. She wants to be loving towards him but whenever the topic of sexuality comes up, she feels compelled to remind him that she still believes homosexuality is a sin.

Rhea's feelings were hurt by a comment from another member of her small group. She doesn't say anything about it, though, and forces herself not to cry because she knows the group will just tell her to forgive and move on.

Roy has faithfully led his congregation for over 25 years but internally he feels empty and hopeless. He's ashamed for not being joyful and worries that if he tells anyone at church about his depression, they'll ask him to step down from leadership.

Morna leads and attends church events several times a week but always leaves feeling drained and exhausted. She's an introvert who needs a lot of alone time, but she feels compelled to keep trying to the endless social energy that her church seems to expect.

Jordan has spent years trying to figure out the cause of her constant body pain and fatigue. The doctors can't find any medical cause and Jordan is starting to feel like she's crazy.

Reflect

Do you ever have trouble identifying or understanding your feelings?

How often do you make decisions based only on what's "right" and "wrong"? What are the risks of that?

How much time have you spent exploring your unique identity? Is there any reason not to do that now?

What did your religious group teach about emotions like anger, hurt, or sadness? How were you encouraged to deal with them?

Have you ever noticed physical symptoms that seemed to be connected to stress or emotional pain?

Relationship Dysfunction

Many religious trauma survivors struggle to navigate relationships in healthy ways after being in high-control groups that have normalized dysfunctional relationship patterns. These groups often reinforce loyalty by making members feel like they'll only be safe and understood within the group.

Common forms of religious trauma relationship dysfunction:

- **Peer Policing**: Feeling responsible to monitor one another's behavior, hold each other accountable, or report rule breaking to authorities.

- **Social Anxiety**: Fear of being judged or excluded, high rejection sensitivity, social avoidance, loneliness, performative relationships, and lack of vulnerability in relationships.

- **Codependency**: Excessive inter-reliance, helping, or enabling that's driven by guilt and obligation.

- **Enmeshment**: Overidentifying with the group, devaluing our privacy and autonomy, and having difficulty separating our own thoughts, feelings, and needs from others in the group.

- **Trauma Bonding**: Feeling obligated to protect and be loyal to people we've experienced trauma with or oversharing (trauma dumping) as a means of bonding.

- **Authority Fawning**: Excessively pleasing, submitting to, honoring, or asking permission from authority figures.

- **Authority Defiance**: Feeling contempt for authority figures, distrusting the intentions of authorities, and refusing to obey rules.

Practical Examples:

Whenever Judy tells people what's going on in her life, she feels like they're going to judge her or get her in trouble. As a result, she tends to get defensive and over-explain her choices even when it's not necessary.

When Juan's pastor asks him to lead a new small group, he says yes even though he really doesn't have the time or the desire to do it. He tells himself that it's what's best for the group even though he feels trapped and resentful.

Elena hates confrontation but whenever she sees a friend making a poor choice, she feels convicted to point it out to them and spare them from consequences. While it repeatedly creates conflict, she's glad it at least spares her from the guilt of possibly letting her community down.

After Darren's church hires a new senior pastor, he goes above and beyond to shower him with compliments, gifts, and favors to make him feel welcomed and appreciated. When the new pastor forgets to thank Darren for a small favor, Darren spirals into panic and starts planning how to get back into the pastor's good graces.

Julia feels dishonest if she doesn't tell her small group about every temptation she feels during the week. She's afraid that someone else in the group will sense that she's holding something back and call her out. Even when she doesn't act on her bad thoughts, she believes that keeping any secrets from the group will ruin their deep connection.

Reflect

What relationship dynamics were normalized in your religious group? Do they seem healthy? Why or why not?

What's your definition of codependency? Did that show up in your religious group?

Do you get socially anxious? If so, what do you usually assume other people are thinking of you?

How do you typically respond to people in authority over you? Is that similar or different from the way you responded to your religious leaders?

Take Inventory

It's time for our first self-inventory. There will be several of these throughout the book to help you identify and reflect on areas in need of healing. These inventories aren't quizzes, so there aren't any right or wrong answers. You won't get a score or a diagnosis at the end. The goal is just to raise your awareness and offer you direction in your journey of healing.

The Religious Trauma Inventory on the next page is a checklist of common beliefs that religious trauma survivors hold. On their own, none of these statements would qualify as religious trauma. However, if multiple statements reflect your current or past beliefs, you've definitely had some adverse religious experiences. As you go through the list, take note of any threat responses or body sensations that might be clues about how religious trauma has and may still be impacting you.

Religious Trauma Inventory

Put a check by the statements that reflect what you feel **now** or **have in the past**.

- ☐ I'm in danger of being excluded from the afterlife.
- ☐ Someone I love might be excluded from the afterlife.
- ☐ The end of the world might happen at any moment.
- ☐ It's my responsibility to tell non-believers the truth.
- ☐ Evil spirits want to hurt, tempt, or possess me.
- ☐ Non-believers want to hurt, tempt, or seduce me.
- ☐ I might commit evil ("sin") without realizing it.
- ☐ God will punish me for making mistakes.
- ☐ God has total control over my life.
- ☐ God designed a clear system of right and wrong.
- ☐ My salvation depends on me doing things right.
- ☐ Bad things won't happen to me if I'm good enough.
- ☐ I'm a naturally bad ("sinful") person.
- ☐ I'm a naturally selfish ("prideful") person.
- ☐ I deserve punishment for being the way I am.
- ☐ There's something wrong with me spiritually.
- ☐ My well-being isn't a priority to God.
- ☐ My value comes from serving other people.
- ☐ I need to work to make up for my failures.

- [ ] My body's natural instincts are wrong.
- [ ] I shouldn't trust my emotions.
- [ ] I should deny my sexual urges or attractions.
- [ ] Masturbation is disgusting or perverted.
- [ ] I should resist the temptation of money or ambition.
- [ ] I should always be joyful or grateful.
- [ ] I shouldn't allow myself to be angry.
- [ ] I shouldn't have doubts about my faith.
- [ ] My identity should be based on my religious beliefs.
- [ ] I should always be loyal to my religious group.
- [ ] People are watching to see if I'm a true believer.
- [ ] I should always confess my failures ("sins").
- [ ] I need to be forgiven by God for my failures ("sins").
- [ ] I need God's permission or approval before I make decisions.
- [ ] I should never be resentful of other people.
- [ ] I should always forgive people who hurt me.
- [ ] I should always serve others, even when I'm tired.
- [ ] I should always submit to people in authority.

Reflect

Were any of the symptoms of religious trauma surprising to you? Which ones? Why?

If you checked some of the symptoms of religious trauma, were you already consciously aware of them? Have you ever been in denial about them?

Have any of your symptoms gotten better over time? Have any gotten worse?

How would you encourage someone else who is experiencing these symptoms?

What would it sound like to offer compassion to yourself?

Chapter 3: High-Control Religious Groups

You've probably noticed my use of the term "high-control" when referring to religious groups that inflict harm. This is because the common thread among most religious trauma stories and cult experiences is a control-oriented group dynamic.

Religious groups that maintain their power through highly controlling teachings, expectations, and hierarchies are more likely to traumatize their members in the process. Any time multiple members of a religious group exhibit signs of trauma, it's a serious warning sign that some of the group's ideologies or practices aren't healthy.

In this chapter we'll explore some of the nuances of high-control groups (including groups that are run by well-meaning leaders). We'll also investigate some of the most common forms of control that religious groups can wield over their members and why they're harmful.

Good Intentions

Many religious leaders have positive intentions and are sincere in their beliefs. This does not, however, guarantee a positive outcome or absolve them of responsibility for the unintended impacts of their words and actions. This tension is a major reason why many religious trauma survivors don't acknowledge what they've been through.

It's easy to accuse someone of abuse if we believe that they knowingly acted with bad intentions. It's much harder to place blame or responsibility on someone who genuinely believed that their actions were going to help others. These situations call for empathy and curiosity that extends to both the alleged abuser and the alleged victim.

Denial is not helpful, however. A leader's devotion to a good cause is not what determines if the people under their leadership have been traumatized. Some of the most devastating events in history are evidence of this. This means that we can't just turn our heads the other way if a group or its leaders have positive intentions.

Reflect

How often do you think religious group leaders are consciously aware that they're harming their members? Why?

Have you ever chosen not to speak up about something because you felt like the person responsible didn't mean to do harm?

Do you think sincere religious leaders should be accountable for the trauma that happens under their leadership?

Is there value in raising someone's awareness about the unintended impact of their actions?

Identifying Patterns of Abuse

Trauma recovery research validates the importance of survivors acknowledging and naming the abuse they've experienced. When someone is wounded, they have to acknowledge and assess the wound before they can treat it properly. Identifying patterns of abuse helps us understand how we've been wounded and some possible reasons why.

Survivors of interpersonal abuse (aka. domestic violence) have helped identify some common controlling patterns of abuse. Research on cults and high-control religious groups shows a lot of the exact same abuse patterns. This means that many of the power and control tactics that are used in abusive relationships can easily be applied in religious settings.

Unfortunately, the intimidating spiritual status of religious leaders and the perceived high spiritual stakes can amplify the effects of power and control tactics in religious groups. This raises the risk of abuse and exploitation substantially.

> Secrecy and silence are an abuse perpetrator's first line of defense.[7]

---

7 Herman, J. (1993) Trauma and Recovery.

Power + Control Dynamics

The Power and Control Wheel, created by the Domestic Abuse Intervention Project[8], is an incredibly helpful tool for understanding the dynamics at play in abusive relationships. It's widely used by therapists, social workers, and advocates to raise awareness and empower victims to address abusive patterns. Each spoke of the wheel describes a different form of power and control that makes a victim feel trapped in a relationship with their abuser.

When it comes to religious abuse, learning about power and control tactics is equally helpful for raising awareness and spotting negative patterns. I'm certainly not the first to do so, but below is my version of the power and control wheel, adapted to the religious trauma experience. Each category describes a way that religious groups can use power and control to keep their members submissive and loyal to the group. As you read each section below, try to be curious and listen to what your body has to say.

---

8 Domestic Abuse Intervention Project (1993) The Duluth Model: The Power and Control Wheel.

Religious Power + Control

Coercion + Threats

Group can maintain control through threats (either explicit or implied). Members are coerced by their fear of practical and spiritual consequences. Nonbelievers may also be coerced to join the group for the same reasons.

Examples:

- Threats of judgement or punished by God or group leaders

- Threats of being kicked out of the group

- Threats of public shaming

- Threats of hell or eternal torment

- Threats of eternal separation from loved ones

- Threats of temptation or harm by evil spirits/forces

- Threats from non-believers

Spiritual Intimidation

Claiming to have a direct connection with a higher power is incredibly intimidating and can inspire unquestioning submission. Spiritual claims might be about the belief system, the religious leaders, or the group itself. This often includes condemnation of all other belief systems and justification of the group's right to enforce their rules on outsiders.

Examples:

- Claims that the group's beliefs are the ultimate truth

- Claims that the group isn't subject to secular authorities

- Claims that leaders have spiritual authority or a divine calling

- Claims that group members are superior to nonbelievers or have the right to rule them

- Claims that the religious text is perfect or inerrant

- Claims that the group's practices are superior to other religious traditions

Emotional Abuse

This abuse tactic disempowers people by decreasing their confidence in their own worth apart from the group. Members who have been repeatedly shamed are much more likely to submit to leaders who appear to be more enlightened.

Examples of religious emotional abuse:

- Setting unrealistic spiritual expectations

- Suppressing and shaming emotional responses

- Shaming and villainizing nonconformity

- Name-calling ("sinner," "apostate," "heretic")

- Devaluing self-care and healthy boundaries

- Villainizing self-confidence ("pride")

Isolation

Cult control techniques almost always involve cutting off the group members from outside support. This prevents them from hearing things that contradict the group's ideology or raising awareness about problematic practices.

Examples:

- Limiting access to outside resources (healthcare, education, etc.)

- Condemning the use of secular media

- Controlling communication within the group

- Discouraging relationships with nonbelievers

- Inciting fear of external threats or agendas

- Dehumanizing outsiders

Minimizing, Denying + Blaming

This common abuse tactic, often called "gaslighting", allows abusers to maintain control by making their victim doubt their own perceptions and opinions. This establishes the abuser as the only one who can accurately assess reality and make valid decisions.

Examples:

- Invalidating members' complaints

- Denying that mistreatment occurred

- Justifying mistreatment with good intentions

- Blaming victims for causing their own mistreatment

- Using spiritual bypassing (see Chapter 6)

- Requiring forgiveness or reconciliation regardless of the circumstances

Loss of Autonomy

Groups may use transparency and a lack of privacy to produce conformity. Suppressing personal agency and discouraging critical thinking makes members reliant on the leaders.

Examples:

- Requiring submission to group leaders

- Telling members to consult leaders before making decisions

- Requiring regular confessions

- Encouraging members to police and report on each other

- Villainizing self-trust and intuition

Defining Gender + Sexuality

This control tactic uses patriarchal views to create strict expectations, enforce conformity, and isolate power to an elite few.

Examples:

- Setting explicit or implicit gender roles for men and women

- Enforcing cisgender and heterosexual norms

- Villainizing LGBTQIA+ identities and behaviors

- Shaming or excluding members who express themselves in non-conforming ways

- Denying women or queer people access to positions of leadership

Economic Control

Many groups profit economically from their members by requiring or strongly encouraging them to donate time and resources for the sake of the group.

These practices also force members to rely financially on the group so they're less likely to leave.

Examples:

- Requiring tithing or donations

- Mandating particular money management techniques

- Discouraging saving or investing money in outside systems

- Demanding trust in God's provision

- Shaming the enjoyment of worldly things

- Limiting the education or employment status of certain members

Reflect

Which categories of the Religious Power + Control Wheel stuck out to you? Why?

What experiences have you had in groups, jobs, or families where power and control were used against you?

What explanations have you heard people use to justify their exploitation of power and control?

How do you think people get lured into controlling systems to begin with?

The Cycle of Abuse

Another well-known psychology tool that explains an important pattern in abusive relationships is The Cycle of Abuse[9]. This simple but profound model shows the sequence of events that repeat in abusive relationships and keep victims trapped. The four stages in the Cycle of Abuse are the following:

Stage 1: Tension Builds

The victim senses the abuser's agitation and starts walking on eggshells to avoid a confrontation.

Stage 2: Incident

The abuser finally explodes with some form of emotional, physical, or sexual abuse.

Stage 3: Reconciliation

The abuser apologizes, makes excuses, blames the victim, and makes promises that things will change; the victim accepts.

Stage 4: Calm

There's a "honeymoon phase" as the abuser showers the victim with affection, the incident is forgotten, and everything seems fine. Eventually, though, the tension begins to build again, and the cycle continues.

As with the Religious Power and Control Wheel, below is my adapted version of the Cycle of Abuse to reflect abusive patterns that can play out in religious groups.

---

9 Walker, L. (2017) The Battered Woman Syndrome.

The Cycle of Religious Abuse

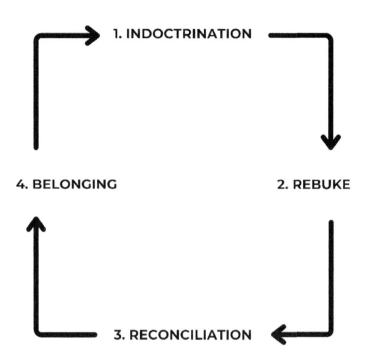

1. INDOCTRINATION

2. REBUKE

3. RECONCILIATION

4. BELONGING

Stage 1: Indoctrination

The cycle begins with relative calm as the group member is taught the group's rules and expectations. As they try to fit in, they slowly begin to sense growing tension underneath the group's ideology. Seemingly loving messages are mixed with expectations of compliance and threats of consequences. The group member starts walking on eggshells hoping to avoid upsetting the group leaders or God.

Stage 2: Rebuke

The tension finally erupts as an abusive incident occurs, often involving public shaming or harsh rebukes for failure to follow the rules. This may include accusations of a lack of faith, required public confession, punishment ("church discipline"), threatened exclusion from the group, or demotion from leadership. The incident can be a single event, or it can be a series of smaller events.

Stage 3: Reconciliation

After the abusive incident, the leader(s) seek to repair the group bond by explaining, justifying, or denying what happened. Often the incident is blamed on the member's behavior or lack of faith. Leaders will typically suggest that the abuse need not happen again as long as the member repents and behaves correctly. Expectations of forgiveness and reconciliation are emphasized so that members will re-commit to the group.

Stage 4: Belonging

Once the uncomfortable incident is over, the member is showered with love and "unconditional" acceptance. Leaders will normalize the previous stages of the cycle and may offer perks or status to the member who has proven their devotion. The group seems safe, even utopian in this classic honeymoon phase.

And Repeat....

Eventually, the euphoria begins to wear off and the group member begins to notice the tension building again. The leaders might warn against becoming complacent or preach about staying vigilant against evil. The cycle of religious abuse repeats.

Reflect

Which stage(s) of the Cycle of Religious Abuse stuck out to you the most?

Have you ever wondered why abuse victims stay with their abusers? What is your perspective on that now?

Have you ever overlooked something harmful or unhealthy in a religious group? If so, what motivated you to do so?

Take Inventory

Time for another self-inventory. The High Control Group Inventory on the next page is a checklist of religious or spiritual teachings that are common in high-control groups. They reinforce conformity, submission, inter-reliance, and fear of outsiders as means of control.

As always, take note of any threat responses or body sensations that come up as you read the list that might be hints about the control level of your current or former religious group. Individually, these teachings may not qualify as religious abuse, but if multiple statements align with a group's doctrine, it would likely be considered a high-control religious group.

High Control Group Inventory

Put a check by the statements that reflect what your group **teaches, demonstrates, or implies**.

- ☐ Our teachings are the ultimate truth.
- ☐ Our teachings are the only path to true happiness.
- ☐ Our group is a utopian community.
- ☐ Our sacred texts are perfect and indisputable.
- ☐ Our leader(s) have special spiritual authority.
- ☐ Our rules are a higher authority than secular laws.
- ☐ Those who reject our teachings or leave our group will face judgment.
- ☐ Those who accept our teachings will be eternally rewarded.
- ☐ We have a special purpose from a higher power.
- ☐ Our group can achieve things that defy science.
- ☐ Humans are fundamentally broken/inadequate without our teachings.
- ☐ Human instincts are evil and can't be trusted.
- ☐ We must enforce our rules on nonbelievers for their good.
- ☐ We have special rules regarding sex that nonbelievers don't understand.
- ☐ Those who defy our sex and gender norms are deviant or dangerous.
- ☐ We use special words/language that nonbelievers don't understand.

- ☐ Evil forces and nonbelievers want to corrupt or harm our members.
- ☐ Evil forces and nonbelievers want to corrupt or harm our children.
- ☐ Negative life events are a form of discipline from a higher power.
- ☐ Personal suffering is a sign of spiritual weakness.
- ☐ Mental illness is a sign of spiritual weakness.
- ☐ Doubting our teachings is a sign of spiritual weakness.
- ☐ Women in our group must submit to men.

Our members are expected to:

- ☐ Limit or cut off relationships with nonbelievers.
- ☐ Recruit nonbelievers into the group.
- ☐ Avoid literature/media that contradicts our teachings.
- ☐ Attend group meetings regularly.
- ☐ Make regular financial contributions.
- ☐ Volunteer their time to the group.
- ☐ Confess temptations and failures to the group.
- ☐ Report other group members' disobedience.
- ☐ Submit to the group's discipline.
- ☐ Forgive and reconcile with other group members.
- ☐ Prioritize the groups' needs over their own.

Reflect

How did you feel while going through the High Control Group Inventory?

Did you ever felt threatened, isolated, or shamed by a religious group?

How have high-control group dynamics impacted your behaviors?

Have you ever perpetuated abusive systems in a religious setting? If so, what were your reasons?

What changes could religious leaders make to minimize the risk of religious abuse?

Chapter 4: Childhood Religious Trauma

When a child grows up in a high-control religious group, the impacts can be uniquely harmful. Early childhood is when our cognitive, emotional, and social development is most important, so a controlling or abusive system will directly interfere. When childhood development is combined with trauma, the damage is especially complex.[10]

This chapter will expand on the religious trauma symptoms that we discussed in Chapter 2, focusing on how children born and raised in abusive religious systems can be impacted.

> **Developmental Trauma** is "exposure to multiple, cumulative traumatic events, usually of an interpersonal nature, during childhood which results in developmentally adverse consequences."[11]

---

10 Abrams, Z. (2021) Improved Treatment for Developmental Trauma.
11 Van der Kolk, B. (2014) The Body Keeps the Score.

Fear + Anxiety

Children generally don't develop the ability to think in abstract terms until around 12 years old12. For neurodivergent brains, this ability may develop even later. When adults teach abstract ideas to children who are still in the concrete thinking stage of development, there can be some major misunderstandings and unintended consequences.

Abstract religious ideas like sin, hell, or the end times can create intense fear in children who aren't developmentally equipped to handle them.

Before they develop abstract thought, children can't tell the difference between concrete reality and things like symbols or metaphors. In other words, they take things literally. Their brains aren't equipped to process abstract threatening ideas without them possibly triggering visceral panic.

For this reason, many children who are taught complex religious doctrines at an early age develop intrusive anxious thoughts. This might lead to perfectionism, fear of their own minds, or fear of non-believers. Additionally, they may have extreme anxiety or panic related to supernatural threats like hell, Satan, demons, or possession.

---

12 Piaget, J. (1971) The Theory of Stages in Cognitive Development.

Reflect

What scary religious ideas (if any) do you remember learning about as a child?

Do you remember having any intense worries, nightmares, or panic attacks as a child? If so, what were they about?

How did people in your religious group usually respond when you were feeling anxious?

What are some abstract religious ideas that could be terrifying to someone with concrete thinking?

Shame

Children often respond to high-control environments with a strong sense of shame. Many kids in these settings will believe that they are "bad" because of their inability to meet the high expectations of the group. This is especially true in religious groups that teach that humans are born evil or sinful. While an adult might be able to accept this belief and still feel confident in their worth, a child won't have a sense of worthiness to fall back on.[13]

The self-criticism, learned helplessness, and low self-trust that are part of a typical religious trauma response are magnified in children. These experiences can make it extremely hard for them to feel confident about themselves, even as adults.

> Children with religious trauma may never remember a time when they didn't have a critical voice in their head accusing them of being bad and worthless.

Unfortunately, some religious groups actually teach parents to discipline their children using shame. Some common shame-based phrases used by parents or religious leaders are, "If you love God, you'll do what's right," "You do bad things it makes God sad" or "Being selfish is a sin". These admonishments might be well-intentioned, but they teach a child that any imperfect behavior might reflect on them as a person.

---

13 Van Deusen & Courtois. (2015) Spirituality, Religion, and Complex Developmental Trauma.

When a child is shamed or punished for parts of their natural identity, they quickly internalize the belief that they are bad. A child's gender identity, sexuality, personality, intelligence, and other capabilities are easy shame targets in groups that prioritize conformity. Research shows that LGBTQ+ children who are shamed in non-affirming settings are much more likely to experience self-hatred and suicidal ideation[14]. This is just one of many statistics that show how toxic shame can be to children.

---

14 Blosnich, et al (2020). Sexual Orientation Change Efforts, Adverse Childhood Experiences, and Suicide Ideation and Attempt Among Sexual Minority Adults.

Reflect

Did you feel like a "bad" kid when you were little? If so, what contributed to that belief?

What did your parents use to motivate you to act the way they wanted?

What religious or spiritual teachings contributed to how worthy of love you felt as a kid?

Did you ever have difficulty telling the difference between your identity ("a bad kid") and your behavior ("a bad choice")? Why?

Rigid Thinking

The development of curiosity and critical thinking skills are an essential part of early childhood. When kids encounter new things, it's normal and healthy for them to ask questions, explore ideas, and try to understand things in different ways. These skills build their confidence in their ability to think, learn, and solve problems.

When high-control groups teach rigid thinking patterns, it impairs a child's cognitive development. This deprives the child of opportunities to practice flexible thinking and trains them to ask fewer questions.

Children raised with rigid doctrine have more difficulty distinguishing opinions from facts and often reject ideas simply because they're new or unfamiliar.

Reflect

As a child, were you often encouraged to do your own independent exploring?

How did people in your religious group respond when you asked questions about their teachings?

How were you taught to determine what was true when you were a kid?

Suppression

Another essential stage in early childhood is the development of autonomy. In order for a child to feel confident and safe, they need to be allowed to have their own feelings, preferences, and opinions. They need to learn that they have the right to make decisions for themselves, to give consent, or to say "no" to things. When a child isn't given autonomy from an early age, they grow up feeling powerless.

Children raised in high-control religious groups aren't given the choice to opt out of the group. Many of them grow up feeling obligated to participate in beliefs and practices that they didn't get to choose. More and more of their autonomy is taken away as they are expected to conform to their group's rules and norms.

Lack of autonomy is even more pronounced in groups that demand obedience and submission from children. In an attempt to make children believe the "right" things and to protect them from "bad" influences, many groups have strict rules that isolate and control their children. This can involve monitoring of a child's education, media consumption, free time activities, friendships, clothing, and more. Each of these forms of control takes away a child's ability to think and make decisions for themself.

Autonomy isn't just about external choices, though. Many high-control religious groups directly or indirectly pressure children to adopt an identity that reflects the group's ideals. This is typically communicated through rigid expectations about values, gender roles, sexuality, and personality types. This means that children aren't free to fully explore and express their natural identities.

Many children in high-control religion grow up trying to mold themselves into whatever the group seems to want instead of learning about their own identity. This low self-awareness makes it hard to figure out what they want or don't want in life. They struggle to make choices that lead to genuine fulfillment because they're living according to who they think they "should" be, not who they actually are.

Reflect

Were there times in your childhood when you felt forced to do things you didn't want? What were the circumstances?

How difficult is it for you to figure out what you want? Is that a skill you were taught in childhood?

Did you ever get punished as a child for trying out new ways of expressing yourself?

Did you ever feel pressured to change something about yourself to fit in with your religious group? How did it go?

Relationship Dysfunction

In early childhood, we each develop an attachment style that sets our expectations for all future relationships[15]. Attachment styles form based on how we connected with our caregivers as infants. A child whose physical and emotional needs were consistently met by their caregivers will usually develop a secure attachment style, meaning they trust that their relationships with others in the future will be safe and rewarding[16].

Attachment styles are the relationship templates that we instinctively expect our future relationships to follow.

Misattunement happens when our emotional needs aren't noticed, validated, and responded to by others. When a child and parent are misattuned, the child feels rejected and alone.

Insecure attachment styles form when a child experiences neglect or mistreatment from their caretaker. The lack of relational stability early in life creates insecurity in future relationships. This can result in clinginess, keeping others at arm's length, or alternating between the two extremes.

Attachment Style research is relevant to children raised in abusive religious settings too. Early experiences with highly controlling caregivers can

---

15 Abrams, et al. (2013). Attachment Theory.
16 Bowlby, Frey, & Ainsworth. (1953) Child Care and the Growth of Love.

create an expectation of judgment and unsafety in future relationships. To better explain these dynamics, I'll outline the three insecure attachment styles.

Anxious-Preoccupied Attachment Style

This attachment style develops when a child's caregivers are inconsistent in responding to the child's needs. If the caregiver(s) is occasionally intrusive or controlling but disengaged at other times, the child learns to constantly monitor their relationships in order to get their needs met. Those with an anxious attachment style are preoccupied with seeking affection and reassurance in their relationships, often seeming clingy and overly dependent on others.

Avoidant-Dismissive Attachment Style

This attachment style occurs when a child's caregiver is misattuned to the child's emotional needs. Even if the child's physical needs are met, when a caregiver is emotionally distant, the child learns that they can't rely on others for affection, security, or comfort. This often results in patterns of holding others at arms' length, avoiding commitment, and being overly independent.

Disorganized Attachment Style

This style develops when a child is fearful because their caregivers are abusive or unpredictable. The child learns that they can't feel truly safe with people they depend on. While the child may continue to seek affection from their volatile caregiver, they also must develop defense mechanisms to keep themselves safe. Those with disorganized attachment styles tend to alternate between anxious and avoidant behaviors, sometimes sabotaging their relationships with mixed messages.

In high-control religious groups, the role of "caregiver" extends beyond a child's parents. Religious leaders, other group members, and even God often take the role of caregivers. Many children raised in high-control religion grow up viewing God as a parental figure who is emotionally unattuned, inconsistent, or abusive[17].

When these complex relationship dynamics play out in a tight-knit group, children are deeply affected. They may feel guilty for being hurt or disappointed and may compulsively seek to appease caregivers in order to get affection. Some detach emotionally after feeling powerless to get the affection and acceptance they need.

---

17 Cherniak, et al. (2021) Attachment Theory and Religion.

Reflect

What did your religious group teach you to expect in relationships?

When you felt a strong emotion as a kid, what kind of responses did you expect from the adults around you?

As a child, what was your view of God like?

Did you ever view God as volatile, punitive, or inconsistent? If so, how did that impact you?

Take Inventory

If you grew up in a high-control religious group, you may have internalized some harmful beliefs about yourself, your spirituality, and the world. The Childhood Religious Messages Inventory on the next page is a list of harmful spiritual messages that can cause serious developmental trauma for children.

While these beliefs don't guarantee that you have religious trauma, they significantly raise your risk and impact your self-worth, sense of control, and autonomy. As you read this list and think about how religious teachings impacted you in childhood, be very kind and gentle with that younger version of you who may still be looking for safety and reassurance.

Childhood Religious Messages Inventory

Put a check by any beliefs that you held as a child.

- ☐ I was born bad.
- ☐ God knows all my thoughts.
- ☐ Satan knows all my thoughts.
- ☐ God watches everything I do in private.
- ☐ God will only forgive me if I'm sorry.
- ☐ Nonbelievers will be tortured in hell forever.
- ☐ If I have doubts, it means I'm not saved.
- ☐ I should know how to fight for my beliefs.
- ☐ My body is bad and will make me sin.
- ☐ My body could make someone else sin.
- ☐ Being proud of myself is wrong.
- ☐ Being angry is wrong.
- ☐ Thinking about myself is selfish.
- ☐ God will punish me by making bad things happen to me.
- ☐ Having sex is wrong.
- ☐ Touching myself (masturbating) is wrong.
- ☐ Being gay or transgender is wrong.
- ☐ I'm supposed to get married and have kids when I grow up.
- ☐ I'm supposed to forgive anyone who hurts me.
- ☐ I'm supposed to show physical affection to anyone who wants it.
- ☐ I'm supposed to ask permission before I do anything.

- [ ] I'm supposed to obey all adults.
- [ ] I should bring my unsaved friends to church.
- [ ] I can only wear clothes that my group tells me are ok.
- [ ] Secular books, TV, and music are dangerous.
- [ ] It's dangerous to be friends with non-believers.
- [ ] When I'm sad or angry, praying or reading the Bible should make me feel better.
- [ ] Demons can control or possess people.
- [ ] God can heal people if we have enough faith.
- [ ] God will answer my prayers if I have enough faith.

Reflect

If you grew up in religion, would you consider it high control? Why or why not?

What did your religious group tell you about your worth as a human? Did that depend on your behaviors?

Did you ever feel like you were a "bad" kid? How did religious teachings influence that?

How do you think the religious teachings you heard in childhood are impacting you today?

Chapter 5: Systemic Religious Abuse

More research is needed to understand the connection between religion and systemic abuse. The data we have so far suggests that people in religious groups are at higher risk for abuse, exploitation, and discrimination but these experiences are significantly under-reported. Victims who report religious abuse are frequently invalidated, ignored, or encouraged to seek reconciliation with their abusers.

To wield power and control, leaders of high-control groups rely heavily on hierarchy. When those at the top of the hierarchy have unchecked power, they're put in a position where abuse and exploitation can occur without meaningful consequences. While not all leaders intend to use their power in exploitative ways, harm can still inadvertently be done.

Although abuse, assault, and exploitation can happen anywhere there's an imbalance of power, its prevalence in high-control religion should make it a top concern for both religious and non-religious people. Fortunately, our culture is becoming more aware and less tolerant of abuse across the board. Numerous groups and individuals are launching new investigations into claims of abuse that until recently, had been ignored. Let's explore a few of the most prevalent hierarchies in mainstream religion.

Leadership Elitism

The hierarchy in high-control religious groups is maintained, in part, by strict rules about who is eligible to be in leadership. Gender, sexuality, race, economic status, and marital status are often part of the criteria. Unsurprisingly, women, children, people of color, the queer community, and other underrepresented groups are the least likely to be in leadership and the most likely victims of systemic abuse.

Hierarchical control is (in part) maintained through the consistent elitist treatment of a group's leaders.

In most high-control groups, those who are in leadership get special treatment because of their status. When a belief system teaches that leaders are chosen or appointed by God, it adds an additional layer of spiritual intimidation.

Unfortunately, elitist criteria and the spiritual status of leaders create systems that are much easier to exploit. Many religious leaders are so trusted by their group that their behaviors are not scrutinized. Their choices regarding money, relationships, and ethical matters are rarely questioned, making it easier for them to do harm (intentionally or unintentionally) without accountability.

The perceived spiritual status of religious leaders is a common reason abused group members choose not to make formal reports or press charges. Victims are often told to trust and submit to the wisdom of their leaders without question, even if the leaders have a conflict of interest. Naturally, this paves the way for repeated exploitation.

Reflect

How were the leaders in your religious group treated? Was it different from how regular group members were treated?

Have you ever seen a religious leader escape the consequences of their actions due to their spiritual status? If so, how did that feel?

Have you ever been hurt by or felt pressured to submit to a leader who didn't seem to have your best interests at heart?

Patriarchy, Sexism + Purity Culture

Most modern-day cultures are firmly founded in patriarchy, a gender-based hierarchy that many take for granted. Some religious groups take it a step further by claiming that humans were divinely created to embody patriarchal ideals. For this reason, male and female members of most high-control religious groups are treated very differently and required to meet different standards.

Women, children, and gender non-conforming people land at the bottom of the patriarchal hierarchy. They are valued less, given less freedom, and expected to submit to the men in power over them. As we discussed in the previous chapter, patriarchal systems remove autonomy from children at an early age.

Many women are discouraged from seeking higher education, working outside the home, or making non-traditional choices regarding marriage and motherhood. As a result, many women feel trapped by their forced dependence on male spouses, fathers, or leaders, all while bearing the bulk of domestic tasks and childrearing.

Women are often expected to dress and behave in ways that align with the group's ideal of femininity. Beginning in early childhood, girls are celebrated for traits such as gentleness, nurturing, compliance, and submissiveness. When girls or women express strong opinions or non-traditional preferences, they are often shamed, criticized, or even excluded from the group.

Sexism in high-control religion is often evident in the lack of female, trans, or non-binary representation in leadership. Groups that only allow men to hold leadership positions tend to have other harmful patriarchal practices. Terms like "complementarianism," "family values," and "the head of the household" are often used in connection with sexist policies.

Men are adversely impacted by sexist ideas too. In patriarchal systems, men are expected to be strong, hardworking, and emotionally disengaged. This makes it extremely difficult for them to feel safe resting, admitting weakness, asking for help, or expressing vulnerable emotions. The more men attempt to fit a skewed patriarchal view of masculinity, the more repressed and dysfunctional they become.

Most high-control religious groups have strict rules regarding sex, sexual attraction, masturbation, pornography, marriage, and expectations of sex in marriage. Some groups even discourage men and women from being friends with one another or being alone together under any circumstances. These policies create heightened anxiety about any perception of sexual impropriety (i.e. "the appearance of evil".)

Purity Culture is a religious ideology founded in patriarchy that shames and/or forbids sexual activity, especially outside of monogamous heterosexual marriage.

Patriarchal control is implicit in the ideology about chastity until marriage, especially when it focuses on female virginity. This is evident in the lack of focus on male virginity. Beginning in childhood, girls are taught to wear modest clothing and are made to feel responsible for preventing their male peers from being sexually tempted[18]. As a result, many females in purity culture report hypervigilance about protecting their sexual purity and fending off hypersexualized boys and men.

Research among adults of any gender raised in purity culture shows a high incidence of sex-related anxiety and sexual dysfunction[19]. Many women experience Vulvodynia, chronic physical pain during sex. When sexual assault happens in purity culture, victims are very unlikely to report or even talk about the assault due to fear that they will be blamed or silenced (more on this later).

Similar to sexism, men are negatively impacted by purity culture too. Intense shame regarding sexual desire, sexual acts, and masturbation, causes many men in high-control groups to repress their sexuality in unhealthy ways. Research supports the idea that this kind of repression leads to secretive or addictive sexual behaviors due to extreme fear of being judged and condemned.

---

18 Denney, et al. (2018) Child Sexual Abuse in Protestant Christian Congregations.
19 Azim, et al. (2021). Epistles of Dyspareunia: Storying Christian Women's Experiences of Painful Sex.

Reflect

What did your religious group teach were the ideal traits of men and women?

Did you experience the impacts of sexism in religion? How did it impact your social relationships?

Have you ever felt shame for not living up to your own expectations of your gender? Where did those expectations come from?

What did your religious group's ideal family look like?

Do you think your current views on gender are shaped by patriarchy? If so, how could you change that?

What religious messages did you hear about the topics of sex, marriage, masturbation, or pornography?

Do you often feel shame, guilt, or fear when thinking about or talking about sex?

What are some of the reasons you've heard religious groups use to justify purity culture messages?

Have your views on sex changed? If so, have your guilt and shame also changed? Why or why not?

LGBTQ+ Abuse

An all-too-prevalent form of religious trauma is the systematic oppression and exclusion of the LGBTQ+ population. Due to the emphasis on compliance and conformity in high-control belief systems, members who don't identify as cisgender and heterosexual are often abused and villainized.

Not all queer oppression is overt. Religious groups that may not seem "high control" still suppress LGBTQ+ identities by teaching and reinforcing the belief that being queer is sinful, deviant, or depraved. Some claim that queerness is an offense to God or simply "not God's best".

Religious efforts to villainize and suppress the queer community don't just impact churchgoers. The United States is currently fighting a large-scale battle about the legal rights of LGBTQ+ people in non-religious contexts[20].

Conversion practices are intended to convince or force LGBTQ+ people to change their natural identities and conform to cisgender and heterosexual norms.

Conversion practices, which have been present in religious groups for centuries, require queer people to simulate heterosexuality, commit to a life of celibacy, and/or conform to traditional gender roles. Both formal and informal versions of conversion practices are extremely damaging and dangerous. In many religious

20 Human Rights Campaign: Roundup of Anti-LGBTQ+ Legislation

groups, refusal to conform can result in shockingly inhumane punishments and social isolation.

A recent study among gay, lesbian, and bisexual people showed that being subjected to conversion "therapy" resulted in a 92% greater chance of considering or attempting suicide[21]. As with any kind of identity suppression, attempting to change a person's core identity through the use of conversion practices is coercive, abusive, and ineffective.

Some countries and states have legally banned conversion practices, but sadly, it's still federally legal in the United States. Numerous advocacy groups, including the Trevor Project and the Human Rights Campaign, are trying to change this, however[22].

In recent decades, millions of cisgender and heterosexual people have chosen to leave their religious groups because of the exclusion or mistreatment of LGBTQ+ people. After becoming aware of the harm happening to their queer friends and family, they've chosen to make a stand. As a result, an increasing number of religious groups and denominations have publicly changed their stances on homosexuality and gender identity.

---

21 Blosnich, et al. (2020) Sexual Orientation Change Efforts, Adverse Childhood Experiences, and Suicide Ideation and Attempt Among Sexual Minority Adults.
22 The Trevor Project (2023) Ending Conversion Therapy

Reflect

What did your religious group teach about homosexuality? What about being transgender or non-binary?

If you're in the queer community, how have religious groups and teachings impacted you? If you're not, how do you think those things might have impacted you?

When the LGBTQ+ community was mentioned in your religious group, how did other members usually react?

Have your views on LGBTQ+ identities changed? If so, what prompted that?

Racism

It would be impossible to document the overwhelming evidence of racial exploitation and abuse that has been done in the name of religion. Most of history's bloodiest race wars were fought over religion (e.g., the crusades). People groups all over the world have been colonized, enslaved, and exterminated by religious groups.

Historically, religious groups have justified human rights violations by claiming to have a **divine right** to rule or enslave people of other ethnicities.

In less overt forms, people of color are abused or exploited in religious communities due to racist doctrine being taught. Evangelistic religious groups who believe they're called to bring their religion to other cultures often enact patterns of "white saviorism"[23]. While not all missionary work is harmful or exploitative, many well-intentioned missionaries have done damage to cultures that they don't understand.

As a white woman and child of former missionaries, I'm very aware of my limited perspective on this topic. Instead of offering my own commentary on racism and religious abuse, I'd encourage you to speak to someone with first-hand experience or read/listen to the many incredible books and podcasts on this topic. Awareness is the first step toward advocacy.

---

23 Jun, et. Al. (2018). White Jesus: The Architecture of Racism in Religion and Education.

Reflect

What was the racial diversity of your religious group? Were people of color in positions of leadership?

What messages did you hear about foreign missions, particularly to poor or non-white countries?

Do you see any connections can you see between religion and racism?

What kinds of covert or overt racism have you seen in religion? Did your religious leaders try to justify it somehow?

Clergy Sexual Abuse

Sexual abuse in religious settings is a devastating reality. It definitely isn't a new phenomenon, but it's gained a lot of public attention in the past few decades. As our culture has become more aware of sexual abuse and power dynamics (see the #MeToo movement), there have been a growing number of survivors who are speaking up about sexual misconduct in religious settings.

In recent years, both religious and non-religious organizations have launched research studies to better understand the prevalence of this issue and what we can do to stop it. Unfortunately, because of spiritual intimidation and the imbalance of power, there are many survivors who still don't feel safe to speak up. This means the statistics we currently have probably don't accurately reflect the scope of this problem.

Religious groups have a long history of mishandling cases of clergy sexual abuse[24]. Among adult women who report sexual abuse by clergy, less than 10% have received help and support from their congregation and about 50% of those victims report being blamed for the abuse and ostracized by other church members[25].

An overwhelming majority of victims who report sexual abuse to church leadership are **ignored, invalidated, or accused** rather than helped.

24 Guidepost Solutions Independent Investigation Report (2022).
25 Pooler & Barros-Lane. (2022) A National Study of Adult Women Sexually Abused by Clergy.

Historically, religious leaders accused of sexual abuse have rarely been held accountable legally, personally, or professionally. Recent inquiries such as the Guidepost investigation into the Southern Baptist Convention's handling of sexual abuse allegations, reveal how often church leaders have been excused from consequences and allowed to continue in their roles as pastors[26].

The spiritual authority of religious leaders that I've written about several times already seems to be a common theme in these cases. According to research in 2019, religious leaders who perpetrate child sexual abuse consistently use their unquestioned spiritual status to gain the trust of their victims and the children's parents[27].

These are some sobering facts and statistics on clergy sexual abuse:

- Most perpetrators of child sexual abuse in religious settings are men in positions of leadership such as pastors or youth ministers.[28]

- At least 3% of women in religious groups report they've been sexually assaulted by clergy.[29] There are likely many more who do not reported it.

- About 8% of church attendees are aware of sexual misconduct that has happened in their congregation.[24]

---

26 Guidepost Solutions Independent Investigation Report (2022)..
27 Raine & Kent. (2019) The Grooming of Children for Sexual Abuse in Religious Settings.
28 Denney, et al. (2018) Child Sexual Abuse in Protestant Christian Congregations.
29 Chaves & Garland. (2009) The Prevalence of Clergy Sexual Advances Towards Adults in Their Congregations.

- 92% of sexual advances made by religious leaders are done in secret to someone they are not in a romantic relationship with; 67% of perpetrators are married to someone else at the time of the assault.[25]

- Most clergy sexual assaults happen on church property, at off-site church-sponsored activities, at the perpetrator's home, or at the victims' home.[24]

- Child grooming in religious settings often begins long before the abuse; physical contact begins with non-sexual touch that progresses over time to sexual touch, so the victim is unaware that the behavior is inappropriate.[30]

- Underreporting of clergy sexual abuse is most pronounced among underage boys.[31]

---

30 Raine & Kent. (2019) The Grooming of Children for Sexual Abuse in Religious Settings.
31 Isely & Isely. (1990) The Sexual Abuse of Male Children by Church Personnel: Intervention and Prevention.

Reflect

What reasons do you think religious organizations might have for denying accusations of clergy sexual assault?

Have you heard about or experienced inappropriate sexual contact with a religious leader? If so, how was it handled?

Do you think religious groups are more likely or less likely to tolerate sexual abuse than secular organizations? Why?

Chapter 6: Spiritual Bypassing

Spiritual Bypassing, a term coined by John Welwood in the 1980s, describes a pattern of sidestepping emotionally complex issues with simple spiritualizations[32]. The intention behind spiritual bypassing is usually positive. These spiritual catchphrases are meant to offer comfort or perspective when life is difficult or confusing. They're often too simple to be satisfying, though, and become toxic when they're overused or applied in the wrong circumstances.

> Spiritual bypassing focuses on explaining and responding to the world through an **exclusively spiritual lens**.

Usually, we aren't explicitly taught how to use spiritual bypassing. Rather, we learn these coping strategies over time when we hear them used repeatedly in our religious groups. We are slowly trained to deal with difficult experiences by quoting church-sanctioned catchphrases that help us explain hard things and avoid discomfort.

Although these phrases try to quickly address hard topics, they inadvertently teach us to filter out uncomfortable information and push down emotions that need to be processed. These spiritualized platitudes might seem nice at face value, but they

---

32 Wellwood, J. (1984) Toward a Psychology of Awakening.

quickly become problematic when no other cognitive or emotional processing is done.

The Impact of Bypassing

Long-term cognitive or emotional avoidance eventually robs us of the ability to cope with stress in healthier ways. When spiritual bypassing is used, the person on the receiving end often feels invalidated, dismissed, or even blamed for their struggles. Habitual spiritual bypassing, therefore, plays a part in many of the signs and symptoms of religious trauma that we discussed in Chapter 2.

When a religious group member has a painful experience, a strong emotional reaction, or a contradictory opinion, others in the group might gravitate towards spiritual bypassing as a solution. While the intentions behind this are usually positive, most spiritual bypasses are focused on suppressing, avoiding, and detaching from pain while reinforcing a group's doctrine.

The solutions that spiritual bypassing offers are **too simple to be satisfying**. They become toxic when they're overused and applied universally.

When we habitually use spiritual bypassing to cope with difficulties in our lives, we get better and better at denying reality and suppressing our emotions. It inadvertently teaches us to detach mentally and emotionally from difficult things, lean into magical thinking, practice toxic positivity, and villainize normal, healthy emotions.

Dissociation

A common trauma symptom that's often closely linked to spiritual bypassing is a sense of disconnection within oneself. It can happen when we're in intense distress and it makes us feel detached from our feelings or experiences.

> **Dissociation** is a coping mechanism that helps us deal with extreme stress by cognitively disconnecting us from reality.

To protect us from danger, our brains can temporarily block out things that might get in the way of our survival. Sometimes it can shield us from the full emotional impact of a situation so we can do what needs to be done. Like any coping mechanism, though, it can become counterproductive. Even if dissociation has helped in the past, it becomes unhelpful when it's overused in inappropriate contexts. It might rescue you from temporary distress, but habitual dissociation will rob you of being fully present for what happens in your life.

Extreme forms of dissociation like Dissociative Identity Disorder (DID) are very rare. The most common forms of dissociation are much less dramatic. Typically, it happens when the stress of our circumstance exceeds our ability to cope, causing parts of our mind to temporarily shut down. Outwardly we may appear to be functioning normally, but inwardly we're not aware of our authentic reactions to the situation[33].

Some common signs of dissociation include:

- Mind going blank or feeling spaced out

- Emotional numbness or detachment

- Out-of-body experiences

- Auto-pilot behaviors

- Few or no memories of a stressful event

- Seemingly unprovoked panic attacks

- Poor awareness of body needs and sensations.

Here's a brief example of how dissociation might look in religious setting:

Jerri is on a church committee tasked with handling recent allegations of sexual assault within the church. No matter how hard she tries to pay attention to the victim's testimonies, her mind keeps going blank and she struggles to remember anything that was said.

---

[33] Carlson & Putnam. (1993) An Update on the Dissociative Experiences Scale.

Reflect

Is dissociation something you may have experienced before? If so, what situations triggered that response?

How could spiritual bypassing increase the risk of dissociation?

Did your religious group teach you to be detached from some painful experiences?

What are the pros and cons of being fully present in a stressful situation?

How might someone know if they have an unhealthy habit of dissociating?

The Core Messages of Spiritual Bypassing

Spiritual bypassing isn't specific to any faith or ideology. It happens in religious and non-religious groups all over the world. Regardless of the group's specific words or phrases, spiritual bypassing relies on several "universal" messages that stay surprisingly consistent across traditions. Below are four of the main messages communicated through spiritual bypassing, how they're used, and why they can become problematic.

Supernatural Explanation

We use this type of spiritual bypassing when we're trying to make sense of life in an over-spiritualized framework. The essential message is, **"There's a spiritual explanation for everything."** When we have complex experiences, whether they're positive or negative, spiritual people often feel motivated to find supernatural explanations rather than natural ones.

When we view the world through this lens, we can easily fall victim to confirmation bias. Eventually, every fortunate event appears to be evidence of our spiritual beliefs and every negative event seems to be a force of evil that must be resisted. Jumping to spiritual conclusions is sometimes innocuous, but a lot of unnecessary anxiety and rigidity can come from it.

On a deeper level, this bypass trains us not to think critically or question things we don't understand. When we habitually rely on supernatural explanations for things (miracles, spiritual warfare, the power of prayer, etc.), we stop being curious about the natural world. This can cause false certainty, lack of personal responsibility, and paranoia about supernatural forces of evil.

Divine Purpose

We usually rely on this spiritual bypass to offer perspective and reassurance when we face things that are difficult to accept. The main message is **"Everything is part of God's plan and will be used for the greater good."** For many spiritual people, suffering feels easier to bear if they believe it's part of a grand design or has a spiritual purpose that couldn't have been achieved otherwise. It offers them a way to accept what they're going through.

While focusing on acceptance or trying to find a "silver lining" might seem positive, this message often makes us feel invalidated and shamed for not having a more spiritually mature perspective. It can also make us feel like we don't really have control over our lives because everything that happens is preordained.

The flawed logic behind this spiritual bypass can suggest that suffering is a necessary evil for good things to happen. It implies that God knows we're going to suffer and chooses not to stop it so he can carry out his plan. Feelings of hurt, abandonment, and powerlessness are all natural responses to this belief.

In extreme cases, this bypass is used to justify abuse or exploitation that happens while we try to bring God's plan to fruition. By bypassing the inner turmoil that we would naturally feel about harming others, we can excuse it in the name of the "greater good". In other words, "the end justifies the means."

Spiritual Edification

The message of this spiritual bypass is, **"There's always a spiritual lesson to be learned."** Driven by our desire to learn and grow, it often prompts self-assessment and self-improvement. In spiritual communities, this message is used to warn each other to be humble, listen to instructions, and stay on the right track.

While looking for opportunities to grow is generally positive, constantly monitoring for spiritual lessons that we or others need to learn can quickly become unhealthy. It can be a weapon of spiritual abuse when we interpret any misfortune as evidence of someone's spiritual failure. This is particularly damaging when a tragedy or a physical or mental illness is viewed as punishment for spiritual weakness.

In high-control groups, spiritual edification pressures members into constantly striving for perfection and submitting to the group's discipline. Their members are expected to continuously find new spiritual insights, feel convicted about their failures, confess, repent, and recommit.

Spiritual Stoicism

This spiritual bypass is usually labeled as "encouragement" and is used as a quick solution for anyone experiencing uncomfortable emotions. The message is, **"True believers don't need to be afraid, angry, or sad."** When someone's struggling with anxiety, grief, or depression, instead of taking time to sit with them and empathize, it's easier to tell them they simply don't need to feel upset.

Although it's meant to be comforting, this message unusually makes us feel even worse. It suggests that if we're spiritually mature, we'll be calm, grateful, and joyful, no matter what. On top of what we're already going through, it adds shame for not feeling completely at peace with our circumstances.

This pressures us to put on a brave face and downplay how hurt, angry, or sad we are. The more we suppress our appropriate emotional reactions, the more detached become. This causes a wide range of dysfunction including avoidance, denial, emotional numbness, lack of empathy (for us and others), and in extreme cases, dissociation.

Take Inventory

If you've spent any amount of time with spiritual or religious people, you've likely encountered spiritual bypassing. You may not have been adversely impacted by it, though, or may have interpreted the core messages differently from what I've described in this chapter. You're free to explore and validate however it impacted you personally.

The inventory on the next page includes some specific examples of the spiritual bypassing that's often used in Evangelical Christian settings. If any of these phrases have been spoken to you in the past, reflect on how it felt to hear that in the moment and notice how you feel about it now.

Spiritual Bypassing Inventory

Put a check by the statements are frequently used in your religious group. Feel free to add any that are missing.

Supernatural Explanation

- ☐ It's a blessing.
- ☐ It's a miracle.
- ☐ It's a sign.
- ☐ Our prayers have been answered.
- ☐ God healed you because of your faith.
- ☐ We're fighting a spiritual battle.
- ☐ Evil spirits are trying to tempt us.
- ☐ Angels are protecting us.
- ☐ God has provided a way.
- ☐ Other:_____
- ☐ Other:_____

Divine Purpose

- ☐ Everything happens for a reason.
- ☐ God works in mysterious ways.
- ☐ Everything works together for our good.
- ☐ The Lord will provide.
- ☐ When God closes a door, he opens a window.
- ☐ He won't give you more than you can handle.
- ☐ Our faithfulness will be rewarded in heaven.
- ☐ We can't fail if God's on our side.
- ☐ Other:_____

- ☐ Other:_____

Spiritual Edification

- ☐ God must be trying to teach you something.
- ☐ You should pray about it.
- ☐ Don't lean on your own understanding.
- ☐ Don't be wise in your own eyes.
- ☐ Money is the root of all evil.
- ☐ Pride goes before the fall.
- ☐ Love the sinner, hate the sin.
- ☐ Confess your sins and you'll be forgiven.
- ☐ Don't let your anger cause you to sin.
- ☐ Other:_____
- ☐ Other:_____

Spiritual Stoicism

- ☐ Be joyful in all circumstances.
- ☐ Count your blessings.
- ☐ Lay your burdens down.
- ☐ Lay your worries at God's feet.
- ☐ Let go and let God.
- ☐ This too shall pass.
- ☐ Forgive and forget.
- ☐ There's no need to mourn; that person's in heaven now.
- ☐ There are no tears in heaven.
- ☐ Other:_____
- ☐ Other:_____

Reflect

What did you feel as you read the examples of spiritual bypassing?

Are there positive elements in those phrases? If so, how could they be communicated without bypassing?

How have you personally been affected by spiritual bypassing?

Do you use ever use spiritual bypassing to cope? What's the core message?

Do any of your religious trauma symptoms seem linked to spiritual bypassing? How?

PART TWO: RECOVERY TOOLS

Congrats, you made it through Part One! The rest of this book will focus on practical tools for religious trauma recovery. As you read and reflect, remember the importance of curiosity, self-compassion, and non-judgment. If you notice unwanted thoughts and feelings, there's no need to be angry at yourself or give up on the healing process. If you feel overwhelmed, it's all right to take breaks, get support, or even pause while you find a trauma therapist.

Chapter 7: Stages of Trauma Recovery

Many in the trauma counseling field refer to Judith Herman's three stages of trauma recovery as a helpful guide[34]. The stages include establishing safety, remembrance and mourning, and reconnection. These stages don't always go in sequential order, however. People recovering from trauma will often bounce between the stages several times as they heal. (Similar to Kübler-Ross's five stages of grief which also don't go in any particular order.)[35]

The rest of this book will focus on my adapted version of the stages of recovery with a specific focus on religious trauma. The five elements are:

1. **Deconstruction** (addressing cognitive dissonance)
2. **Safety + Autonomy** (creating a lifestyle of psychological safety)
3. **Remembrance + Reframing** (telling and validating your story)
4. **Self-Understanding** (getting to know yourself authentically)
5. **Healthy Relationships** (reimagining how to relate to others)

Before we dive into those stages, however, I will briefly address a couple of common barriers to recovery and explore why they get in the way of healing. Religious trauma survivors who grow self-

---

34 Herman, J. (1993) Trauma and Recovery.
35 Kübler-Ross, E. (1969) On Death and Dying.

awareness and self-compassion can make their recovery journey a lot easier.

Self-Awareness

High-control religion often teaches us that we can't or shouldn't trust our own minds and bodies. This creates a major barrier to recovery, though. It keeps us from acknowledging and validating our subjective experiences, thoughts, feelings, and needs.

Most religious trauma survivors find it hard to let themselves **think and feel independently** without shutting down, being self-critical, or feeling guilty.

If like me, you were taught that thinking about yourself is "selfish" or that your mind will try to deceive you, this is an important barrier to address. Learning to validate your thoughts and feelings will probably be challenging. The good news is that when you begin to establish trust in yourself, you'll find it easier and easier to make confident decisions.

Self-Compassion

The opposite of self-compassion is shame, an emotion that Brene Brown defines as the "intensely painful experience of believing that we are unworthy of love and belonging."36 Recognizing shame is very important in the religious trauma recovery process because if we don't address it, it blocks us from feeling capable or deserving of the healing that we need.

> **Shame** is the demoralizing belief that we are broken and fundamentally inadequate.

An important distinction is the difference between guilt and shame. Many high-control religious groups teach members that guilt means they have done something that displeases God. Unfortunately, shame-based beliefs often are disguised as conviction or guilt. The core difference between these two ideas is that guilt is about behavior, while shame is about our core view of ourselves.

A key step in addressing shame is noticing the shame-based self-talk that you've internalized. Next, you can start practicing replacing it with a more empowering and compassionate alternative. These are some examples of shame-based beliefs contrasted with self-compassionate beliefs. Notice which ones resonate with you.

---

36 Brown, B. (2012) Daring Greatly.

Take Inventory

The Shame vs. Self-Compassion Inventory on the next page has two columns; the first includes shame-based beliefs that drive self-hatred, self-neglect, and self-abandonment. The second column is a list of alternative beliefs about self that are much more compassionate.

The goal of this exercise is to help you identify your own shame-based beliefs and learn some alternative ways of viewing yourself that are more realistic and less destructive. If you read any statements in the self-compassion column that seem false to you, imagine saying them about someone else and see if they still feel untrue.

Shame vs. Self-Compassion Inventory

Shame	Self-Compassion
I'm defective or broken	I've been hurt but I'm not broken
I'm not good enough	I'm worthy of acceptance
I can't trust myself	Getting to know myself will build self-trust
I'm not loveable	I'm worthy of love even though I'm imperfect
My needs aren't important	My needs matter equally as much as everyone
I'm too emotional / I'm too sensitive	My feelings matter even when they aren't convenient
My thoughts/ideas are embarrassing	My thoughts are worth sharing even if they're not revolutionary
My personal goals are embarrassing	It's worth pursuing the things that motivate me
I'm lazy	Everyone needs rest and relaxation, including me
I'm selfish	Everyone needs to take care of themself, including me
I'm prideful	It's healthy to be proud of myself
I'm a burden	Relying on others is normal and healthy
My mistakes are humiliating	Making mistakes is normal and I learn from them
I need to apologize for being myself	I only need to apologize when I've said or done something I regret

I deserve punishment	I can appreciate and accept compassion
Criticism proves that I'm a failure	A criticism of my behavior doesn't reflect my worth
My body is disgusting	My body is normal and it's worth caring for
No one will ever understand me	If I give others a chance to get to know me, maybe I'll be pleasantly surprised

Reflect

What stood out to you in the comparison between shame vs. self-compassion statements?

Did you resonate with anything in the shame column? If so, how long have you felt that way?

What religious teachings or experiences may have contributed to your shame?

Which statements in the self-compassion column feel the most difficult for you to accept?

Do you have other shame-based beliefs that are worth replacing? If so, what's a reality-based but positive alternative?

Chapter 8: Deconstruction

In the next chapter, we'll start tackling the emotional and social elements of trauma recovery. First, however, we'll start where a lot of religious trauma survivors begin: the cognitive side. This is because when someone is detaching from an abusive system, it can be less painful (initially) to start by addressing logical fallacies instead of vulnerable emotions. If you identify as more a "thinker" than a "feeler," I have a warning for you, though: cognitive deconstruction is only one part of recovery. The emotional part is still coming.

In this chapter, we will explore some of the important foundations for religious deconstruction. The deconstruction process is particularly challenging for survivors of religious groups that emphasize or require conformity of thought. The ultimate goal of deconstruction isn't to fully accept or reject the belief system, but to assess each element individually without jumping to forgone conclusions.

> **Religious deconstruction** is a process of breaking down and analyzing the various parts of a belief system and its practices.

Cognitive Flexibility

Deconstructing begins with challenging our minds to think outside of the rigid boundaries that we were taught to stay within. This requires us to question our assumptions and biases, a difficult thing to do even without religious trauma. These are some crucial elements of cognitive flexibility.

Accepting Uncertainty

Contrary to what you may have been taught, faith and belief are not founded on certainty. Some degree of uncertainty will always be present in any belief system. Accepting this can relieve a lot of pressure to figure out the absolute truth. Having cognitive flexibility requires you to accept that beliefs will always rely on trust, not certainty.

Listening to Diverse Views

It's easy for us to get trapped in an echo chamber where everyone just repeats what we already believe. The danger of this is that we assume that our echo chamber represents reality instead of a biased sample.

Cognitive flexibility requires us to listen to and consider evidence from all sides instead of rejecting conflicting information prematurely. Fortunately, once we've truly listened to diverse views, we can rest assured that the beliefs we hold on to can stand up to scrutiny.

Spiritual Thinking Errors

Thinking errors are unhelpful or unrealistic assumptions or mental filters that cause us unnecessary stress. They tend to escalate anxiety, resist new evidence, and send us into unwanted repeated cycles. Often thinking errors can be recognized by words like always, never, right, wrong, good, or bad.

Below is a list of some common thinking errors that might impact people from dogmatic religious groups. The purpose of this list is not to discourage you but rather to raise your awareness so that you can begin to change these unhelpful habits. Try to examine your own thinking to identify any of these patterns.

Moralizing

This thinking error involves making inaccurate or oversimplified judgments about what's "good" or "bad," "right" or "wrong".

Examples:

- Viewing opposing ideas as two opposite extremes without nuance or gray area.

- Judging certain emotions "bad" regardless of the context.

- Assuming that people who live in ways that contradict your beliefs are evil or have bad intentions.

False Certainty

This error assumes that your opinions are absolutely correct because you feel strongly about them.

Examples:

- Viewing a subjective belief as an absolute truth that can't be disproven.

- Rejecting valid information because it contradicts your prior opinion.

- Assuming that your beliefs should be universally enforced because you believe them.

- Justifying collateral damage if it's in pursuit of the greater good.

- Assuming a spiritual conclusion and using it as proof that an assumption was correct (ex. the Bible calling itself inspired).

Spiritualizing

This error is when we assume events have spiritual causes or explanations instead of natural ones.

Examples:

- Attributing positive events to divine intervention or miracles.

- Attributing negative events to divine punishment or spiritual warfare.

- Blaming someone's suffering on spiritual weakness.

- Using superstitious rituals to try to control things through spiritual means (ex. praying for safe travels).

- Interpreting adverse events as evidence of religious persecution.

Eternal Focus

This becomes a thinking error when it leads us to neglect current-day concerns by fixating on eternal events or consequences.

Examples:

- Using spiritual bypassing cliches to avoid directly dealing with difficult issues.

- Making life decisions around fear of and preparation for the end times/rapture.

- Assuming that something is predetermined, prophesied, or unstoppable.

Reflect

Do you ever get trapped in these thinking errors? Under what circumstances?

How often do you look for conflicting evidence to challenge your assumptions?

How often do you settle for a middle ground instead of an extreme?

What are some reality-based thoughts you could replace these thinking errors with?

Congruence of Beliefs + Values

As you deconstruct a belief system, you may start to notice that some of those beliefs don't necessarily match up with your personal values. This part of deconstructing, often called differentiation, requires you to separate your individual thoughts and opinions from those of the group. It often brings up a lot of discomfort, particularly if your religious group explicitly or implicitly taught you not to think for yourself.

Discomfort while you're differentiating is important to pay attention to, though! It's probably an indication that you're sensing incongruence - a clash between your beliefs and values.

Incongruence is the internal discomfort we feel when our beliefs, values, and actions seem to contradict each other.

Congruence is the sense of peace we feel when our beliefs, values, and actions are in alignment.

Establishing congruence between your beliefs and values is challenging but very rewarding. You probably have conflicting instincts that are waiting to be understood and reconciled. When you finally start paying attention to the things in a belief system that you're uncomfortable with, you have the power to do something about it.

Later in the chapter, you'll identify some of your core values so you can assess how they match up with the beliefs that cause incongruence for you. This process may prompt you to reassess your values, but it may also prompt you to deconstruct a belief that doesn't fit with your values anymore.

Start this process by paying attention to signs of internal tension. When you notice a belief that consistently provokes internal discomfort or cognitive dissonance, don't push it down. It's time to do some detective work. Ask questions and dig deeper.

> **Ignoring incongruence** rarely makes it go away. Confronting it allows us to work toward resolution.

Beliefs that commonly provoke incongruence include:

- I shouldn't question what's ultimately right and wrong.

- It's my responsibility to make sure the people around me believe the right things.

- People who don't believe in the right things will go to hell.

- God chooses to save some people from hell but not others.

- I must submit to authority figures no matter what they ask of me.

- Evolution and climate change undermine God's sovereignty.

- Gender and sexuality can only be correctly defined in one way.

Reflect

Do you think you've experienced incongruence related to religious beliefs? If so, has it resolved?

Are you currently pushing down any conflicting beliefs and values? If so, what are you afraid will happen if you stop?

How did your religious group respond when members expressed feelings of incongruence?

Elements of Religious Deconstruction

As you investigate your belief system and try to identify sources of incongruence, it may be helpful to have a list of topics to consider. Below is a list of the main elements of religion that people often wrestle with during deconstruction. Each topic will include some questions to help you explore further.

Deconstruction isn't about finding the "right" answers or reaching certainty. The goal is to be **curious** as you search for congruence.

Truth, Good, + Evil

Philosophers and theologians have been contemplating the nature of good and evil for centuries. Deconstructing this category is less about finding definitive answers and more about using curiosity as we explore things like ultimate truth, why suffering exists, and whether humans are fundamentally good, evil, or neutral.

Questions to Explore:

- Is God good? Is God capable of doing evil?

- Does God decide what is good and evil?

- Are good and evil universal or are they subjective?

- How can humans determine what's good and evil?

- Are humans born fundamentally good or evil?

- Are humans sinful or do they just exist in a sinful world?

- Can a bad person become good and vice versa? How?

- Why is there evil, suffering, or pain in the world?

- Did God create the world intending for evil to happen? Why?

Design

This category includes our beliefs about the origin of the world, the fate of the world, the meaning of life, the purpose of human existence, and the extent of responsibility that humans have over our choices. Our beliefs about everything from evolution to the end times fall into this category.

Questions to Explore:

- How did the universe come into being (creation, evolution, etc.)?

- Are world events unfolding according to a greater plan?

- Is God orchestrating world events?

- Is evolution real? Why or why not?

- How important are humans to God's plans?

- Are all humans created equal in value?

- Do humans have agency (free will) over their choices?

- What (if anything) is predestined or predetermined?

- Can humans be held responsible for predetermined actions?

- Did God intend for there to be only two distinct genders?

- Did God intend for humans to be heterosexual only?

- Is each person made exactly as God intended?

- Does God create people and punish them if they don't conform?

Divinity

Not every religious group believes that there is a god or that there is only one God. Deconstructing divinity means investigating the belief system's "higher power" and questioning thinking like the extent of their power, their character, their motivations, their limitations, etc.

Questions to Explore:

- Is there only one God?

- How can we determine who the true God is?

- How can humans learn about God?

- What does God require from humans (if anything)?

- How are good or evil spirits different than gods?

- What is God's character like?

- Is God good, all-knowing, all-powerful, etc.?

- Does God's character evolve as humans evolve?

The Afterlife

Most religious belief systems speculate about what happens to the human body and/or spirit after we die. Deconstructing the afterlife means investigating our assumptions about the finality of death, and deciding what we believe about reincarnation, paradise, eternal punishment, resurrection, etc.

Questions to Explore:

- Do the choices we make in life have eternal consequences?

- What happens to the souls of humans when we die?

- Is there a heaven and hell?

- Does any part of a human get reincarnated?

- Do non-believers get annihilated after death or go to hell?

- Is hell a place of eternal conscious torment?

- What criteria determine what happens to someone after death?

Dominion

Deconstructing dominion means questioning how much power and authority we attribute to the things we believe in. Our assumptions about who and what has the inherent right to power (God, Scripture, religious leaders, chosen groups, etc.) have major implications for how we interact with the rest of the world.

Questions to Explore:

- Does religion hold the ultimate truth?

- Should God's desires be carried out on earth?

- Should religion be involved in politics?

- Is there a God-ordained hierarchy between genders?

- Is there a God-ordained hierarchy between races or classes of people?

- Do humans have authority over the earth?

- Do religious groups or leaders deserve special power?

The Sacred

Most religious groups have practices, objects, and traditions that they consider sacred. Deconstructing the sacred means assessing what makes something sacred, how necessary it is to our beliefs, and how flexible we can be in using it. A few examples are group gatherings, marriage ceremonies, interpreting scripture, and speaking to the divine.

Questions to Explore:

- Why do religions have set practices and traditions?

- How strictly should religious practices be followed?

- Is Scripture sacred?

- Is Scripture inerrant (never wrong)?

- Who has the right to interpret Scripture?

- Do sacred events (miracles, signs, prophecies) ever occur?

- How can a human know what's sacred and what's not?

- Does prayer have a practical impact on the material world?

Reflect

What fears do you have, if any, about questioning your religious beliefs?

Is binary thinking or black-and-white thinking common in your religious beliefs? If so, were you taught to think that way?

Which of your religious beliefs, if any, provoke shame, anxiety, hopelessness, or anger in you? Why?

Take Inventory

Your core values are things that motivate you and give you a sense of meaning. They often change from one season of life to the next, depending on how your perspective shifts. Your values are completely your own and they can bring you a sense of ownership over your life. Doing a values inventory is intended to help you connect with yourself and choose goals for the future.

On the next page there's a list of common core values that people hold. None of them are right or wrong, they're just subjective. As you read through the list, put a check by the ones that stand out to you personally. If you end up checking more than ten, go back and try to narrow it down to your top five values. Remember, your core values don't have to match what you've been told is important in the past.

Core Values Inventory

☐ **Adaptability** — flexibility, accommodation, adjustment

☐ **Ambition** — drive, aspiration, desire

☐ **Analysis** — assessment, evaluation, investigation

☐ **Authenticity** — truth, genuineness, originality

☐ **Ballance** — temperance, moderation, carefulness

☐ **Belonging** — connection, acceptance, community

☐ **Caution** — careful, tentative, thoughtful

☐ **Collaboration** — cooperation, participation, teamwork

☐ **Compassion** — mercy, grace, benevolence

☐ **Competition** — rivalry, contest, controversy

☐ **Consistency** — dependability, stability, predictability

☐ **Courage** — bravery, daring, fearlessness

☐ **Courtesy** — politeness, kindness, deference

☐ **Creativity** — invention, innovation, discovery

☐ **Curiosity** — inquisitiveness, questioning, exploring

☐ **Defiance** — nonconformity, resistance

☐ **Discipline** — restraint, regulation

☐ **Duty** — obligation, responsibility, work

☐ **Empathy** — sensitivity, understanding, inclusivity

☐ **Excellence** — achievement, accuracy, success

☐ **Excitement** — adventure, anticipation, variety

☐ **Freedom** — autonomy, independence, agency

☐ **Gratitude** — thankfulness, appreciation

☐ **Humor** — amusement, levity, sarcasm

☐ **Influence** — persuasion, impact, guidance

☐	Integrity	ethics, honesty, honorability
☐	Intentionality	purposeful, deliberate, mindful
☐	Justice	impartiality, equity, fairness
☐	Logic	reasoning, intellect, deduction
☐	Loyalty	commitment, attachment, allegiance
☐	Nurture	care, soothing, support
☐	Optimism	hopeful, expectant, positive
☐	Order	organization, categorization, systematic
☐	Passion	expression, drama, intensity
☐	Peace	serenity, calm, harmony
☐	Play	enjoyment, fun, amusement
☐	Power	strength, authority, leadership
☐	Practicality	objectivity, groundedness, realism
☐	Productivity	activity, effort, industriousness
☐	Progress	evolution, improvement, advancement
☐	Propriety	poise, decorum, properness
☐	Recognition	respect, esteem, honor
☐	Selflessness	helpful, altruistic, sacrificial
☐	Simplicity	clarity, certainty, plainness
☐	Skepticism	doubt, suspicion, critical thinking
☐	Tolerance	inclusivity, forbearance, non-judgment
☐	Virtue	righteousness, morality, principles
☐	Wealth	abundance, affluence, prosperity
☐	Wisdom	insight, perceptiveness, discernment

Reflect

Do any of your beliefs seem to be incongruent with the core values you chose? If so, why?

Do you think you can change your core values? Why or why not?

Do you think you can change your beliefs?

How can you determine which values or beliefs you might want to change?

Chapter 9: Safety + Autonomy

The safety and autonomy phase of religious trauma recovery is all about establishing and affirming your right to feel comfortable, think for yourself, and make decisions that are in your own best interest. (Remember the trauma alarm signal that we discussed in Chapter 1.) Safety and autonomy require us to listen to our body's alarm signals, investigate the cause, and be willing to confront barriers that are keeping us from feeling truly safe.

Trauma has a way of robbing us of our sense of safety and autonomy, making it difficult for us to feel calm and in control. Before we can heal and move on from trauma, we first need to feel confident that we're free and safe, at least for the present moment. If we're feeling trapped or threatened physically, emotionally, or spiritually, our minds and bodies will keep trying to protect us by staying in survival mode.

Learned Helplessness

Psychological researchers discovered the theory of learned helplessness in 1967 when conducting an experiment. They placed dogs in a cage with a food bowl on the other side and shocked them with an electric current when they first tried to walk to the food bowl[37]. Researchers found that when they stopped using the shocks, the dogs still wouldn't make any effort to get to their food bowl because they had "learned" through previous experience that they were helpless. When they conducted similar experiments with humans, the results were the same.

Learned helplessness is a self-defeating sense of powerlessness that can happen when we've experienced repeated trauma.

Authoritarian systems like over-controlling parents, schools, or religious groups often make us feel like we don't deserve the right to choose things for ourselves or decide what happens to us. Rather than empowering us to make good choices, this kind of control keeps us from figuring out what we need and how to get it. When we are faced with a lack of control for long enough, we unconsciously decide to give up on trying to make our lives better.

When it comes to trauma recovery, learned helplessness has major implications. If our past experiences have taught us that we are powerless to control or change our circumstances, it becomes very difficult to shift out of that mindset. Learned

---

37 Seligman & Maier. (1967) Failure to Escape Traumatic Shock.

helplessness can convince us that we're incapable of making choices that will actually lead to a sense of safety and autonomy. Unfortunately, this leaves us stuck, waiting for others to validate our needs and feelings, give us permission to do things, and advocate for us.

Take Inventory

On the next page is a Learned Helplessness Inventory that has some practical examples of ways that long-term lack of control can impact our lives. As you take the inventory, try to suspend self-judgment and shame. Remember that learned helplessness is a symptom of trauma, not a sign of weakness. The good news is that you can heal and start changing these self-defeating patterns.

Learned Helplessness Inventory

Check the statements below that sound like you.

- ☐ I struggle to find motivation in life.
- ☐ I struggle to set goals for the future.
- ☐ I often predict that I'll fail or be bad at something new.
- ☐ I often assume that I'm going to live an unhappy life.
- ☐ I often assume that my money problems can't be fixed.
- ☐ I often assume that my relationship issues can't be fixed.
- ☐ I often assume I don't have any control over my circumstances.
- ☐ I often wait for someone else to solve a problem.
- ☐ I often give up on things when I face challenges.
- ☐ I'm quick to assume I can't help other people with their problems.
- ☐ I'm quick to write off viable options without considering them.
- ☐ I've stayed in unhealthy jobs for too long.
- ☐ I've stayed in unhealthy relationships for too long.
- ☐ I've repeated my past mistakes before.
- ☐ I sometimes look for "signs" that I should give up on something.
- ☐ I feel powerless to achieve something good.
- ☐ I feel powerless to change my unhealthy habits.

- [ ] I can't really trust my own judgment.
- [ ] I don't feel like I can protect myself from being hurt.
- [ ] I rarely feel capable when starting a task.
- [ ] I need lots of encouragement from others before I make decisions.
- [ ] I feel abandoned when other people don't fix my problems.
- [ ] I rarely think to speak up for myself.
- [ ] I don't usually expect to get what I want in a situation.
- [ ] I don't see the point of complaining about how someone treats me.

Reflect

What stood out to you in the learned helplessness inventory?

Does learned helplessness seem to be interfering with your daily life? If so, how?

What past goals, if any, have you written off or given up on because of learned helplessness?

What does your self-talk sound like when you're struggling with learned helplessness?

What could you try telling yourself instead that would be more helpful?

Self-Trust

Safety and autonomy are both physical and psychological experiences. While getting away from obvious external threats is a priority, internal triggers matter too. Trauma survivors often need to acknowledge internal unsafety before they can shift out of survival mode. For those with religious trauma, there's often an added layer of shame and self-doubt that makes it hard for us to trust our senses.

Learning to trust our feelings and instincts is a skill that many of us have to work on after leaving high-control groups. As a living, conscious being, it's your job to pay attention to what you need, protect yourself from harm, and express what you think and feel.

Every human, **including you**, is allowed to notice when they feel uncomfortable and make changes to establish safety and autonomy.

Take a moment to sit quietly with yourself and affirm that it's okay to listen to and trust yourself. As you do the reflection section below, be ready to offer yourself as much grace and compassion as you would offer someone you love.

Reflect

What did you notice when you affirmed self-trust and honesty about your feelings? (Remember not to judge too quickly!)

Are there drawbacks to being truly honest with yourself about your feelings? If so, what are they?

What are the benefits of affirming that your feelings matter?

Do you think you have a pattern of ignoring, judging, or invalidating your feelings? If so, why?

What emotional reactions or body sensations do you notice when you're in a religious setting?

What emotional reactions or body sensations do you notice when thinking about religious beliefs?

Consent

One of the most powerful and effective ways to increase our sense of safety and autonomy is to prioritize asking for and giving consent. If this term is unfamiliar, consent is the act of giving permission for something to happen to us. It isn't just about asking permission before sexual contact, though. Giving and asking for consent should be a regular practice in a broad range of contexts because it allows each person to decide what they want or don't want to happen to them.

> Consent is how we each demonstrate that we have **ownership** of ourselves.

Think of consent as the language of autonomy. The more explicit consent there is, the more autonomy there is. When we're more intentional about asking others for consent, we usually start feeling more confident in our own right to give or withdraw consent as well.

In high-control systems, consent is rarely valued. Members are expected to participate, serve, or even lead regardless of their personal preferences or level of comfort. In a healthy environment, however, all parties are given the opportunity to opt out of any activity that makes them feel unsafe or uncomfortable.

Take Inventory

On the next page is a Freedom of Consent Inventory that lists practical examples of things that someone with a high sense of personal autonomy would likely believe and demonstrate. Each statement reflects a belief that you deserve respect and expect others to treat you that way.

As you read the inventory, take note if any of the statements sound selfish, bossy, or entitled. If so, that might be a sign that you don't value your own consent as much as you value other peoples' comfort.

Freedom of Consent Inventory

Check the statements below that sound like you.

☐ I verbally ask what other people want instead of guessing.

☐ I verbalize what I want instead of waiting for others to ask me.

☐ I ask for permission before I physically touch other people.

☐ I expect other people to ask permission before they physically touch me.

☐ I feel empowered to stop any physical contact I don't want.

☐ I feel empowered to leave situations I don't want to be in.

☐ I consciously try to respect other people's personal space.

☐ I respect other people's requests about how I treat them.

☐ I respect other people's right to change their minds about what they want.

☐ I feel empowered to change my mind about what I want.

☐ I ask other people if they want my advice before I give it.

☐ I ask other people if they want my help before I give it.

☐ I try to offer multiple options when I'm asking people what they want.

☐ I try not to push other people to give in to what I want.

- ☐ I try not to guilt other people into doing what I want.
- ☐ I try not to scare other people into doing what I want.
- ☐ I feel empowered to ask for more information before deciding what I want.
- ☐ I don't hide things from other people in order to get what I want.
- ☐ I feel empowered to speak up when my privacy isn't being respected.
- ☐ I ask for permission before sharing something private about someone else.

Reflect

What does it feel like when you give consent versus when you don't?

Does your consent seem as important as everyone else's? Why or why not?

What situations or people tend to make you feel like you don't have any choices?

How assertive are you when you need help?

Which religious teachings may have decreased your sense of agency?

Boundaries + Resolutions

It's nearly impossible to establish safety and autonomy without dealing with the unhealthy and unrealistic expectations that other people have for us. Setting healthy limits or "boundaries" is usually the only way to address this problem without completely cutting off contact.

Boundaries are personal policies that we adopt to protect our physical and mental health.

When trying to get out of a high-control religious group (or abusive relationship) that typically has free access to your time and energy, setting some firm boundaries to protect your safety and autonomy is highly significant. If you've ever tried setting boundaries, though, you already know it's not always easy.

A common misconception about boundaries is that they're limits we tell other people not to cross. This approach often causes hurt, frustration, and disappointment, though, because other people often don't understand and therefore, don't comply with the boundaries we set. In fact, the people we need boundaries with the most are usually the least sensitive to our need for more autonomy.

Instead of asking other people to respect and uphold our boundaries and waiting to see if they follow through, a more autonomous approach can really help. I call these self-managed boundaries "resolutions".

> **Resolutions** are things in our control that we choose to do consistently to protect our own well-being.

It's much easier to control and follow through on your own resolutions than it is to make someone else do that work for you. If you decide to go this route, you don't need to ask for others' permission. Instead, you can just inform them that this is something you've decided to do to support your own well-being.

Setting a Resolution

Let's get practical. Below are the main steps for setting an effective and sustainable resolution. Each step has a concrete example of someone putting it into practice. Don't worry - you'll get a chance to practice it for yourself afterward.

Target the Triggers

Setting a healthy resolution starts with identifying the things that commonly trigger feelings of being unsafe or trapped. Try to be curious instead of judgmental as you investigate which people, places, or situations tend to be involved. Once you've narrowed it down, start looking for things that you have control over.

Example:

Jackie has noticed recently that she dreads seeing or talking to her mom. After investigating why this might be, Jackie realizes that ever since she stopped attending the fundamentalist church that she and her mom are members of, her mom has been consistently pressuring her to go back. Nearly every time they talk, her mom brings it up.

So far, Jackie's response has been to either make an excuse ("I'm not feeling well today") or give in and go to church with her mom even though she feels miserable and panicked through the whole service. Jackie decides it's time to come up with a resolution that will make her feel less anxious about talking to her mom and less pressured to go somewhere that makes her highly uncomfortable.

Make a Plan

The next step is to brainstorm about your range of options. Start by making a list of all the various ways you could address the problem without dismissing any of them too soon. Now think about the pros and cons of each option so you can narrow it down and choose the one that seems like it'll be most effective.

Once you have a general idea of what you want to do, put it in the form of an "I" statement that focuses on your behavior, not the other person's. Make a detailed plan of precisely what you're going to do or say the next time the triggering situation happens. If it seems helpful, try practicing your plan with a friend.

Example:

Jackie writes down some options of how she could respond the next time her mom asks her to attend church. She notes the pros/cons of each one as she goes.

- Option 1: She could simply say "no thanks" without offering any kind of explanation. Pros: It's simple. Cons: Her mom might pressure her to explain instead of dropping it.

- Option 2: She could ask her mom to stop pressing her about church attendance but not explain why it matters. Pros: This would be more direct without unnecessary aggression. Cons: Her mom might feel hurt anyway and/or press for an explanation.

- Option 3: She could lie and say she's attending church elsewhere. Pros: Her mom might stop asking. Cons: She'll feel guilty and will have to find a way to maintain the lie in the future.

- Option 4: She could explain to her mom that she doesn't feel comfortable at that church and would like to take a break from attending while she figures things out. Pros: This would be an honest way to get a hard conversation over with and hopefully her mom would stop pressuring her for a while. Cons: It would be a difficult conversation and her mom might not respond well.

- Option 5: She could tell her mom she's an atheist now and is offended by her mom's church invitations. Pros: It would put a quick stop to the invitations. Cons: It would be an overstatement and the aggressive tone would probably wound her relationship with her mom.

After investigating her options, Jackie decides on Option 4. She decides that the next time her mom asks about church, she will say, "I appreciate the invitation, but honestly, I haven't been feeling comfortable at church lately and I've decided to take a break." If her mom gets upset or pushes back, Jackie plans to gently tell her mom, "I love you, but this is still something I need to do to take care of myself."

Put it into Action

The next step is to take action. Your resolution is only going to protect you if you follow through on it. When the situation triggers your feelings of unsafety, it's time to do your best to implement the plan instead of falling back into old patterns. Gently remind yourself why you set this resolution to begin with and try not to let your nerves break your resolve to establish safety and autonomy.

Example:

As Jackie prepares for her weekly phone call with her mom, she rehearses her plan. She repeats empowering self-talk to build her courage, including, "I'm allowed to speak up for myself." and "I don't need my mom's agreement or permission to take care of myself." As she gets on the phone with her mom, she's nervous but determined to stick to her plan. When her mom inevitably asks about church on Sunday, Jackie responds with her prepared statement and then gives her mom a chance to absorb it. Her mom's response sounds confused and a little defensive, but Jackie chooses not to abandon herself by caving. Eventually, the phone call ends.

Assess + Calibrate

Once you've tried out your resolution, reflect on how it went. Assess whether you upheld your resolution or not and identify anything unexpected that happened. If it went as you planned, great! Celebrate that! If not, this is your chance to brainstorm what you can do differently if the situation happens again. Think of small adjustments that might make those barriers easier to address. The goal of this step is not to judge or shame yourself, it's to calibrate your plan to increase the chances of a healthy outcome.

Example:

Jackie congratulates herself for telling her mom that she doesn't want to attend church. Although it didn't go perfectly, she's relieved that she no longer needs to attend church or keep making excuses every week.

She feels hopeful that if future conversations about church are necessary, they'll be a little easier now. As she reflects on her mom's defensive reaction, she reminds herself that it's understandable but not a sign that she's done anything wrong. If her mom brings up the church again in the future, Jackie plans to restate her need to take care of her own spiritual and mental health by choosing not to attend. If her mom continues to challenge it, maybe a longer conversation will eventually be necessary. For now, though, Jackie feels relieved and proud of herself.

Be Consistent

It can be tempting to drop your resolutions for a couple of reasons. The first is that you feel pressured by others to give it up. The second is that the triggering situation starts getting easier for you to handle. Either way, these are signs that your resolution is working. Being consistent in implementing your resolution lets other people know what to expect from you. If they're pushing back, it just means you'll need to continue following through on your resolution until they recognize it as the new normal. If the target situation has already gotten easier to deal with, that means you're doing a great job. Keep trusting yourself to protect your well-being.

Example:

Jackie gets a little pushback from her for a couple of months after setting and sticking to her resolution. Eventually, though, Jackie's mom confronts her with concerns that she's backsliding and wants Jackie to meet with their church's pastor. Although Jackie could give in and start attending church again just to avoid a frustrating conversation, she chooses to give her mom some more information about why she's chosen not to attend anymore. She explains that she feels extremely tense and anxious at that church and doesn't leave feeling spiritually connected. She asks her mom to respect her decision even if she doesn't fully understand or agree with her reasons. Although her mom is sad to hear this, she chooses to stop bringing it up.

Make Your Own Resolution

Think of a relationship or situation where you need to establish more safety and autonomy for yourself. Now's your chance to practice setting your own resolution.

Target the Triggers

What situation repeatedly provokes feelings of unsafety or a lack of autonomy for you?

What patterns or people are usually present in those situations?

What specifically do you feel pressured to do or not do to please others?

What would need to be different for you to feel safe?

Do you feel ready to create a resolution to protect yourself? (If so, keep going. If not, go back through the previous questions.)

Make a Plan

How have you typically responded to this situation in the past?

What do you have control over in this situation that you could choose to do differently? (Write down your whole range of options.)

Which of the options above seems the most likely to lead to a positive outcome?

Is that option realistic and does it prioritize your safety and autonomy? If so, write down your new resolution in the form of an "I" statement that focuses on your choices and behaviors.

What possible barriers could make your resolution harder to uphold? If they happen, how will you respond?

What signal will let you know it's time to implement your new resolution?

If your resolve wavers, what's a helpful mantra you can repeat to yourself? (Now go put it into action!)

Assess + Calibrate

How would rate your current sense of safety and autonomy?

Were you able to follow through on your resolution? Why or why not?

What progress can you celebrate even if it was small?

Did you feel the need to get permission from anyone? Did anyone push back against your resolution? If so, why?

If the situation happens again, what can you do differently, if anything?

Be Consistent

Other than external pressure, is there any reason for you to give up on your resolution?

If you consistently follow through on your resolution, how will that impact others' expectations?

Now that you've practiced implementing your resolution, do you feel an increase in safety and autonomy? If so, celebrate that! If not, what might need to change to make your resolution more effective?

Chapter 10: Remembrance + Reframing

Imagine you're out gardening one day when a particularly aggressive thornbush snags your arm and draws blood. You're busy trying to finish your project, though, so you plan to clean and bandage the wound when you go inside later. As you keep working in the soil, you see some weeding you want to get done too. By the time you finally go inside, you've forgotten all about the wound.

The next morning you wake up to a painful throbbing in your neglected arm. You tell yourself it's just a tiny little wound that'll probably heal if you leave it alone. After continuing to ignore it, the wound on your arm develops an infection, getting more and more painful. If it starts to fester, the wound that started out so small could eventually become life-threatening.

> **Unaddressed trauma** is like an old wound that has never been tended to and can't heal properly.

We can always hope for the best and wait to see if a wound heals on its own, but in most cases, trauma doesn't go away that easily. We often have to do some painful but necessary work to clean out the wound before it can really start healing. This reality is both inconvenient and unfair, but it's been validated by trauma survivors over and over again.

Remembrance

Cleaning out the wound of past trauma begins with acknowledging that we've been hurt and deciding that we deserve to heal. Telling our story is a symbolic way for us to validate that the wound happened, take stock of the damage, and start imagining what healing can look like.

> **Remembrance** is honoring the reality of what you've experienced by telling your story.

A lot of trauma survivors avoid the remembrance stage of recovery because they fear that acknowledging the wound will somehow make it worse. Although telling your story will be painful, the wound was already there. The only thing that will truly make it worse is ignoring it.

As you remember and mourn what you've experienced, you'll need to honor all of it. Some parts of your story might make you laugh, and other parts might make you cry. Some of it will be confusing, uncomfortable, or painful. Try not to edit out the complex range of emotions it brings up.

> Honoring your **full experiences** will be a complex journey of joy, pain, anger, grief, regret, and hope.

Some survivors find it helpful to tell their story out loud to someone supportive. Others prefer to journal about it privately. Some tell their story in small chunks while others tell it all at once. Regardless of who you choose to tell your story, be compassionate toward yourself and reach out for the support you need.

Those who experience complex trauma from multiple adverse experiences often feel the need to retell their story several times. This is normal and usually just means that we're not done fully acknowledging the wound yet. Even though this stage is difficult, there's usually a sense of catharsis that happens when we're done honoring our story.

Perhaps the most important thing you can do when telling your story is to offer compassion and empathy to the past version of you who experienced those things. This is often easier to do when you're telling it to an empathetic listener who can offer validation that what you went through shouldn't have happened.

If you feel guilt, regret, or shame, remember:

You were making the best decisions you could **with the information you had at the time.**

Reflect

Have you ever told the story of your religious trauma to a supportive person? If not, what's been holding you back?

Do you have any fears about telling your story? If so, what do they indicate?

Do you feel like you've fully acknowledged the wounds you experienced in high-control religion yet?

Naming

As we remember our stories, it's important to start using appropriate terms to describe what happened instead of watering it down. It's normal when we experience trauma to downplay the impacts by denying, minimizing, or sugarcoating the truth. This doesn't do justice to our experience and pain, though.

Choosing words like "trauma", "abuse", or "indoctrination" may seem harsh at first, but they're usually more accurate and truthful. Softening our language will only invalidate our own experiences and continue to protect the people who hurt us.

> **Naming** our experiences what they truly were allows us to fully acknowledge the wound and start healing.

When it comes to healing from religious trauma, raising self-awareness is half the battle. Every time we notice echoes of trauma in our thoughts or behaviors, we can try to remind ourselves of the new things we've learned. We can normalize the trauma responses we're having instead of judging ourselves. We can make different choices, speak to ourselves differently, and set different boundaries to slowly change unwanted habits.

Reflect

What are the possible impacts of downplaying your own trauma?

What words do you typically use to describe what you've experienced? Do they tend to minimize or sugar-coat the reality of what happened?

Do you shy away from words like "trauma", "abuse", "assault", or "coercion"? If so, why?

What specific events or patterns might need to be re-labeled now that you're acknowledging the wound?

The Trauma Narrative

Trauma narratives are the stories that we repeat to ourselves about what happened to us and why. Any kind of story comes with implied meanings, morals, or lessons. (For example, the lesson of the story about the boy who cried wolf is that people won't believe you if you make too many false cries for help.)

Our trauma narratives usually contain deeper messages too. In the wake of a traumatic event, we automatically make unconscious interpretations about why it happened and what the "lesson" was. Unfortunately, trauma narratives are rarely helpful because they're so tainted by fear, hurt, and blame.

When we've retold and reinforced our trauma narrative for a long time, it's easy to accept it as the truth, even if it's completely inaccurate or illogical. When we base our thoughts and choices on the distorted "lessons" of our trauma narrative, dysfunction, confusion, and powerlessness start stacking up.

Take Inventory

On the next page is a Trauma Narrative Inventory with a list of very common internal narratives that trauma survivors adopt in order to make sense of what they've been through.

It's completely understandable why someone would believe these narratives. There's often a lot of shame and fear of consequences that make these stories seem true or easier to accept. If you've been telling yourself some of these trauma narratives, that means you've had to cope with invalidation and shame about something that never should have happened to you in the first place.

If you check more than a couple of these statements, it's possible that your negative trauma narratives are causing difficulty in your daily functioning. Therapy with a licensed counselor who specializes in trauma would likely be liberating for you.

Trauma Narrative Inventory

Check the statements below that reflect things you've thought in the past.

- ☐ My experience doesn't count as trauma because it could have been worse.
- ☐ People will assume I think my trauma is worse than other people's.
- ☐ The same thing happened to lots of people so it must not be a big deal.
- ☐ I must have done something to deserve what happened to me.
- ☐ My experience proves there's something shameful about me.
- ☐ It's immature that I'm still upset about what I experienced.
- ☐ The physical and emotional reactions I'm still having are irrational.
- ☐ If I were stronger, it wouldn't have impacted me so much.
- ☐ If I were stronger, it wouldn't have happened in the first place.
- ☐ I can prove that I've moved on by pretending It didn't happen.
- ☐ Calling it trauma would be admitting that I'm permanently broken.
- ☐ There's nothing I can do about it now but move on and try to forget.
- ☐ If no one else remembers it happening, I must have made it up.

- ☐ If I tell other people what happened, they'll blame me.
- ☐ If I tell other people what happened, they won't believe me.
- ☐ If I tell other people what happened, they'll see me as broken.
- ☐ If I tell other people what happened, it will ruin someone else's life.
- ☐ The person/people who hurt me had good reasons or good intentions.
- ☐ The person/people who hurt me couldn't control their actions.
- ☐ My experience made me stronger so I should be grateful for it.

Reframing

Now that you have some awareness of your trauma narrative, it's time to start thinking about reframing it. These are three basic steps to help you get started.

Step 1: Identify It

Examining a trauma narrative is like cleaning out an infected wound to finally get rid of a stubborn infection. The first step is to reflect on the old narrative you've been telling yourself to investigate the unconscious "lessons" you've been believing.

Hopefully, the Trauma Narrative Inventory you just took helped you identify some of the unhelpful beliefs that you internalized because of your trauma. Notice if there were any patterns like shame, blame, or denial. Take a moment to journal about how those negative beliefs are currently affecting you. Do you feel trapped? Helpless? Isolated? How does that prompt you to act? How does it affect your relationships?

Step 2: Challenge It

Now that you've identified the unhelpful trauma narrative and how it's continuing to impact you, it's time to reassess by looking at it from a different perspective. It often helps to imagine a loved one of yours is telling their trauma narrative. Think about how you'd react if you were hearing it for the first time from someone you love.

Instead of defaulting to your old interpretations, examine and question them. Negative core beliefs need to be debunked before you can look at your story in a new light. Keep an eye out for these specific things:

- Automatic shame or self-blame

- Outdated assumptions you don't believe anymore

- Thinking errors that are common for you

- Unfair or unrealistic expectations you have for yourself

- Premature conclusions about what it all means

If you notice any inaccurate or unrealistic interpretations, write them down and imagine how you would respond to a loved one if they said those things. Gently address each problematic interpretation with the same amount of grace you would offer your loved one. Even if you're not sure you really believe it yet, start practicing reminding yourself of the alternative perspective.

Step 3: Reframe It

With practice, telling yourself a more empathetic and validating version of your trauma narrative can lead to incredible relief. It won't erase the reality of what happened, but it can clear out the unnecessary clutter of shame, blame, and self-hate that often accompany our trauma narratives.

This reframing takes time and practice, though. You won't be perfect at it immediately but don't give up. Every time you're reminded of the old, self-defeating trauma narrative, you have an opportunity to practice. Try taking a deep breath and intentionally repeating the new story from your new perspective.

Replacing shame-based beliefs with **empathy-based beliefs** makes it possible for us to accept and love ourselves.

Shame about our past reactions and choices will be much easier to understand and forgive if we've worked to reframe our trauma narrative. After we've practiced the new narrative for a while, it becomes easier and feels more natural to care for and be kind to ourselves.

Reflect

What self-sabotaging beliefs are you carrying? What experiences reinforced those beliefs?

Have you given yourself permission to reject religious teachings that are clearly harmful to you? If not, why?

Do you often talk to yourself in harsh or judgmental ways? If so, do you think your religious group taught or encouraged those?

Did you have to learn coping strategies to survive religious abuse? If so, are they still serving you now?

Do you feel like you have the power to change the unwanted thoughts or reactions related to your religious trauma? How would you like to start responding instead?

Chapter 11: Self-Understanding

Self-understanding is an element of trauma recovery that many of us will need to return to multiple times as we grow. It allows us to be authentic with ourselves and figure out why we think and feel the way we do. Best of all, true self-understanding teaches us, often for the first time, how to love and accept who we are.

Religious trauma survivors who were fortunate enough to have a healthy sense of self before joining their religious group might find this process easier. For those were born and raised in high-control religious groups or who stayed in them for many years, this stage will be challenging. It may feel a little like having an identity crisis.

> Self-understanding is the foundation of a **meaningful** life, making healthy choices, forming positive relationships, and having compassion for ourselves.

Many high-control religious groups teach members not to trust their natural inclinations. Although the reasons they give for these teachings differ, the inevitable result is a tighter web of control. People who have been taught to be afraid of looking inward can only build their goals, preferences, and roles on what's been handed to them by others.

Religious teachings that claim that humans are depraved, sinful, or wicked by nature, often point to "deviant" traits or behaviors as evidence. These groups often create an idealized identity for members to strive toward while labeling other identities as "wrong" or "bad". This pushes group members to avoid true identity exploration and focus instead on conforming to the group's ideal.

Those who have spent a lot of time in high-control religion may not even recognize how stunted their self-understanding truly is. They may feel confused about who they are, or angry that they can't force themselves to be different. Fortunately, when we have the freedom to get to know ourselves without shame or pressure to conform, we can finally learn to accept our authentic selves. The process may be disorienting but it has an incredible payoff.

Identity Exploration

Discovering our identity is kind of like venturing into an unexplored map in a video game. When we start out, the map is completely dark and only reveals itself as we explore. Although we can see the parts of the map we've already visited, the unexplored parts remain a mystery until we venture into them. Even when we assume we've seen all the map has to offer, there may still be lots of unexplored territory we haven't even reached.

Exploring our identity map means scoping out unfamiliar territory, listening to our inclinations, and paying attention to the risks and benefits of the new places we find ourselves in. Some new terrain might be scary and uncomfortable. Some places might feel like coming home for the first time. We'll only know what's available to us if we explore.

> Our authentic identity is one that we **choose freely** from the wide range of possibilities that are open to us.

As we set out on our journey of self-understanding, we need to give ourselves permission to leave the tiny area of the map we've been limited to. We'll need curiosity and non-judgment to genuinely consider each path without jumping to outdated conclusions. The things our religious groups would have frowned on in the past are no longer forbidden. We're free to go or stay.

A great first step for mapping identity is learning about our personalities. An easy starting place is to take a personality test such as the Enneagram Personality Test. Don't get too hung up if the results don't sound exactly like you. These types of tools aren't perfect, but they offer us different ways of explaining our behaviors and understanding our natural temperaments.

Subjectivity

It's normal for each of us to have individual preferences about things like relationships, work, food, style, entertainment, etc. We can each be curious about what inspires us and motivates us. We can notice the roles that we tend to take on, the kinds of jobs we enjoy, or the leisure activities we feel excited about[38].

Give yourself permission to have opinions and preferences that are subjective, even if others disagree. **You're allowed to be your own person.**

There are lots of ways to increase self-awareness and build confidence in our own identities. Some great things to try out are traveling, trying new foods, listening to different kinds of music, spending time with diverse types of people, trying different styles of clothing, trying out new routines, and researching new topics.

Whatever you decide to try, the goal is simply to notice what you're feeling (physically and emotionally) without adding any pressure to jump to conclusions.

---

38 Rotter, J. (1954) General Principles for a Social Learning Framework of Personality Study.

There's no need to be ashamed if you discover something you didn't already know about yourself. That's the whole point! Investigate what you're learning about yourself and remember you're free to make whatever choices seem healthy for you.

Reflect

What have you been told in the past about who you are and what your identity is?

Have you ever felt trapped in performing certain identity traits that others expected from you? If so, why?

Can you think of something that you used to like or dislike but changed your mind about? What prompted that realization?

What did your religious group teach you was the "right" type of identity to have? Did you try to conform?

Self-Affirmation

Get in the habit of talking to yourself the way you would talk to someone you love. Be encouraging, compassionate, and patient. This habit will make it much easier to accept yourself for who you are instead of shaming yourself for not being who you "should" be.

If understanding yourself is really difficult, you may benefit from spending some intentional time reflecting, affirming, and reinforcing the parts of yourself that you like. It may seem repetitive, but repetition is the most effective way to change your thinking. Try writing down or speaking the self-affirmations below to yourself.

Examples of Self-Affirmations

"I'm valuable and worth protecting."

"My feelings and needs are important."

"I have the right to feel safe and comfortable."

"I have the right to feel differently than other people."

"I have the right to do what's good for me."

"I have the right to speak up for myself."

"I have the right to rest, relax, and be happy."

Understanding Emotions

Emotions are not good or bad, right or wrong. The way we choose to express our emotions can be appropriate or inappropriate, but the feelings themselves are not wrong. Similar to the way physical feelings inform us what's going in and around our bodies, our emotions give us crucial information. Acknowledging and understanding our emotions is essential to functioning effectively.

Dysfunction is inevitable when we block or invalidate our own feelings instead of taking them seriously. When we try to stop our feelings before we've processed them, they stay trapped inside our bodies, unable to serve their purpose. When we make a healthy habit of naming, accepting, and processing our feelings, we don't just understand them better, we have more control over how we express them.

Every emotion has two things to offer:

INFORMATION about how we're being impacted by our experiences, and

MOTIVATION to take some sort of action.

Keep in mind that emotions, like trauma, are always subjective. What feels like a wound or an injustice to one person, may not feel that way to another. This doesn't mean either person is wrong; it simply means they've had different past experiences that inform how they perceive the current situation.

Survivors of high-control systems often have trouble identifying and understanding their own feelings. If this sounds like you, it may be helpful to read some of the basic, primary emotions and learn what kind of information and motivation they each give us. As you read, try to offer yourself compassion and empathy instead of judgment.

The Basic Emotions

Anger

Information: I've experienced or heard about an injustice.

Motivation: I want to find a way to stop more injustice from happening or at least speak up for the person who was hurt.

Desire / Longing

Information: I've identified something that I want or need.

Motivation: I want to either pursue the thing I desire or find a healthier way to meet that need.

Disgust / Hate

Information: I've encountered something that seems repulsive or toxic to me.

Motivation: I want to either avoid the thing that disgusts me or reassess my biases against it.

Fear

Information: I've encountered something that seems to be a threat to me or my needs.

Motivation: I need to protect myself from the threat (fight, flight, freeze, or fawn) or reassess why it seems dangerous to me.

Guilt

Information: I've done something that goes against my own values or beliefs.

Motivation: I want to either take corrective action or reassess the values and beliefs I'm not living up to.

Hurt

Information: I've experienced some kind of wound that has left me vulnerable.

Motivation: I need to take time to heal from it and possibly set boundaries to protect myself from being wounded this way again.

Joy / Happiness

Information: I'm feeling contentment or enjoyment in something.

Motivation: I want to be fully present for this and continue to seek fulfillment.

Loneliness

Information: I'm missing out on genuine connections with other people.

Motivation: I want to learn how to be vulnerable enough with others so they can get to know me authentically.

Sadness

Information: I'm grieving the loss of or separation from something that matters to me.

Motivation: I need to give myself time to grieve and eventually look for new sources of happiness.

Shame

Information: I've been confronted with my own imperfection or human limitations.

Motivation: I need to either accept my imperfect self by setting realistic expectations or reassess my assumptions about what gives me worth.

Reflect

Which of the emotions listed above seemed hardest for you to connect with?

Which emotions do you tend to shut down rather than letting yourself feel them?

How often do you use your emotions to help motivate you to make healthy choices?

How could naming and processing your emotions help you understand yourself better?

Close your eyes and notice what you're feeling physically and emotionally right now. What information and motivation do those feelings give you?

Chapter 12: Healthy Relationships

Our definition of what's "normal" in relationships is based on our past experiences. If our religious group normalized unhealthy relationship dynamics, we may not even realize there are other, healthier ways of relating to people. This starts with learning how to recognize the difference between healthy and unhealthy relationships. In this chapter, we'll focus on two relationship dynamics in particular: unhealthy codependency and healthy vulnerability.

Codependency

Patterns of codependency almost always develop in high-control religious groups. This is reinforced by teachings about guilt, shame, pride, and selfishness that tell us we need to be rescued by God and accepted by the group. Groups that discourage members from setting boundaries, having privacy, or making autonomous decisions, are essentially enforcing codependency.

> **Codependency** is when reliance or obligation in a relationship cause someone to put up with unhealthy patterns or mistreatment.

In codependent relationships and groups, at least one person is choosing to accept something unhealthy instead of losing the relationship. Usually, they're afraid that without the relationship they'll be helpless, unlovable, or purposeless. When families, partners, or friends have requirements that take away someone's autonomy, they're codependent.

Aside from the coercive pressure of obligation, codependency usually develops along with two other unhealthy patterns: enabling and enmeshment.

When the members of a dysfunctional relationship are desperate to keep the relationship intact, they will go to great lengths to manage each other's problematic behaviors. This often looks like offering endless amounts of help and support in order to keep someone afloat. This is known as enabling.

Enabling is a pattern of rescuing someone from the consequences of their unhealthy choices.

Unfortunately, while the person doing the helping usually has good intentions, the person being enabled loses their motivation to change or take responsibility. This pattern plays out in religious groups when someone with spiritual authority is excused from consequences because the rest of the group relies on their leadership.

The other codependent dynamic that's normalized in codependent relationships is enmeshment. It happens when the people in a group or couple put so much effort into sharing their thoughts and feelings that they lose their sense of individuality. They stop being able to think and act independently.

Enmeshment is when an individual can't distinguish their own identity from others in the relationship.

In high-control religion, enmeshment makes power and control much easier for leaders to wield. It trains group members to mold their thoughts and behaviors to match those of the group. They're often even told that is kind of "unity" is ideal. An enmeshed group identity, however, makes it much harder for someone to feel capable of disagreeing with or leaving the group.

Take Inventory

Time for another self-inventory! The Codependency Inventory on the next page has a list of common thoughts, feelings, and behaviors that show up and can seem normal to someone who has been in codependent relationships for a long time.

This inventory might be uncomfortable for you if you haven't spent much time thinking about how codependency impacts you and your loved ones. Try not jump to self-judgment, though. Awareness of the problem is the biggest step toward recovery.

If you check multiple items on this inventory, I recommend talking to a therapist to get support as you start setting boundaries and prioritizing self-care.

Codependency Inventory

Check the statements below that reflect things you frequently think or do.

- ☐ I often prioritize other people's needs even if I'm neglecting my own.

- ☐ I feel guilty when I have to say no to other people's requests.

- ☐ I volunteer my time even when I'm busy with other things.

- ☐ I show physical affection to others even when I'm uncomfortable.

- ☐ I give money to others even when I'm struggling financially.

- ☐ I sometimes resent other people when I'm doing favors for them.

- ☐ I often pretend I'm not hurt by other people's insensitive actions.

- ☐ I stay loyal to certain people even when they keep hurting me.

- ☐ I feel obligated to forgive people even when they keep hurting me.

- ☐ I often apologize even when I don't think I've done anything wrong.

- ☐ I will ignore physical discomfort if I'm busy helping someone else.

- ☐ I try to spare my loved ones from the consequences of their actions.

- ☐ I often feel responsible for making other people feel happy or calm.

- ☐ I feel hurt when other people choose to keep things private from me.
- ☐ I feel hurt when other people don't anticipate what I need.
- ☐ I feel guilty when I can't anticipate what other people need.
- ☐ I notice my mood shifting to match the people around me.
- ☐ I feel obligated to be the peacemaker when others are in conflict.
- ☐ I feel panicked when there's a disagreement, even if I'm not involved.
- ☐ I often take care of people who can technically care for themselves.
- ☐ I usually get anxious when I have to do tasks on my own.
- ☐ I often worry that I'm upsetting other people without even realizing it.
- ☐ I need other people to tell me if I'm making the right decision.
- ☐ I don't feel confident until I've gotten reassurance from others.

Reflect

When you think about codependency do you typically associate it with religious groups? Why or why not?

What kinds of relationship dynamics were normalized in your religious group?

Do you ever feel selfish when choosing to take care of yourself? If so, did your religious group reinforce that?

Do you ever feel obligated to do things in relationships that you're inwardly resentful about? If so, why do you do it?

Do you ever tolerate mistreatment from other people without speaking up? If so, why?

What boundaries or resolutions could you set to protect yourself from codependent patterns?

Vulnerability

Time to focus on a positive relationship dynamic that's essential to healthy human connection: vulnerability. As the word suggests, vulnerability involves risk because it requires us to intentionally expose our weaknesses to other people. Meaningful relationships can't happen without vulnerability, though.

> **Healthy vulnerability** is the intentional decision to be emotionally honest with people who have earned our trust.

Being vulnerable is especially counterintuitive for those of us who have escaped controlling groups or relationships that weaponized our weaknesses against us. This is why many religious trauma survivors have difficulty trusting and opening up to people without anxiety.

Establishing vulnerable relationships is a sign that we have journeyed far enough through trauma recovery that we no longer need to shut others out to feel safe. This is a big step and it's not an easy one. It puts the responsibility on us to determine slowly and carefully who we're going to trust and then take the risk of offering true vulnerability.

Although it would be nice, other people aren't mind readers. They can't connect with us when we hide our emotions, and they can't meet our needs when we don't verbalize them. Fortunately, once we've chosen to be vulnerable, all we have to do is communicate. When we share our feelings, admit our mistakes, or ask for help, our vulnerability allows us to love and be loved by others[39].

---

39 Brown, B. (2012). Daring Greatly.

Take Inventory

It's time for our very last inventory. The Relational Vulnerability Inventory on the next page lists various practical ways that you can choose to practice emotional vulnerability in your relationships.

Many of these may not feel authentic or comfortable to you yet. If so, that's ok. This is just an opportunity for you to explore all of the possible ways you can allow other people to get to know the real you.

If you notice some ways that you're already showing relational vulnerability, take a moment to celebrate that by telling yourself, "I'm so proud of you for trying to connect authentically with people despite everything you've been through. You're strong."

Relational Vulnerability Inventory

Check the statements below that seem to represent you.

- ☐ I let people know when I want something.
- ☐ I know how to verbalize my feelings to other people.
- ☐ I try to show sincerity when I want to connect with someone.
- ☐ I admit it to other people when I make mistakes.
- ☐ I ask for what I need even if it might be inconvenient.
- ☐ I ask for help instead of waiting for someone else to offer.
- ☐ I ask my friends for favors occasionally.
- ☐ I know how to verbalize to others that I'm uncomfortable.
- ☐ I can hear other people's feedback without getting defensive.
- ☐ When someone's upset with me, I can hear out their concerns.
- ☐ I tell other people when I'm celebrating something positive.
- ☐ I look for comfort from other people when I'm down.
- ☐ I look for empathy from other people when I'm hurting.
- ☐ I can have hard conversations when they're necessary.
- ☐ I openly share my struggles with other people.

- ☐ I try to invite honest feedback from other people.
- ☐ I can openly acknowledge when I'm not good at something.
- ☐ I can openly acknowledge when I don't know something.
- ☐ I can openly acknowledge when I've made a mistake.
- ☐ I sometimes cry in front of other people.
- ☐ I'm okay with not looking my best in front of other people.

Reflect

How safe was/is it for you to be vulnerable in your religious group?

Were your weaknesses ever used against you? If so, how?

Have you ever experienced a trusting relationship where you felt safe being vulnerable? What was/is it like?

Who in your life could you choose to be more vulnerable with?

Chapter 13: Moving Forward

Good job! You've made it through a lot of content, and I hope you're feeling more self-understanding and compassion than you did before. If you find yourself cycling through anger, grief, or depression from time to time, remember that's normal. Instead of beating yourself up for not being "better" yet, remember that you're having an understandable response to a deep wound.

If the content in this workbook was extremely difficult for you to process, that's likely a sign that working with a therapist would be helpful for you. That being said, I know that many religious trauma survivors, myself included, have had negative past experiences with religiously biased counseling.

If you're willing to give counseling another try, I strongly recommend finding a licensed therapist who does not practice from a religious viewpoint. This will decrease the risk that you'll feel tricked, coerced, or triggered by your past experiences.

Tips For Choosing a Therapist

If you're ready to try counseling again or have never tried it before at all, below are some helpful tips for choosing a therapist that fits your needs and some resources for locating them.

Specialty

Identify the specific issues you want to tackle before you start searching for a therapist. While any licensed therapist should be competent in counseling for general issues like anxiety or depression, they aren't all experts on niche topics. Issues like complex PTSD and religious trauma require specialized training. Be wary of therapists who claim to "specialize" in a multitude of different areas.

Therapy Style

Most therapists will advertise the therapy styles(s) they're most comfortable working with. If a therapist says they're "eclectic," it just means they pull from multiple different approaches. Feel free to research online to understand your options. When it comes to religious trauma, research suggests that these modalities are most effective: Internal Family Systems (IFS), Somatic Experiencing, Cognitive Behavioral Therapy(CBT), and EMDR.

Preferences

Some people have specific preferences about their therapist's gender, faith orientation, cultural background, and familiarity with marginalized populations. Although this might limit your options a little, it's worth prioritizing the things that will create a safer therapy environment for you. Most therapists' websites will give you this info but don't be afraid to ask.

Setting

Decide if you want to meet for therapy in person or online. Many therapists have online or hybrid options that allow you to do therapy from home through a HIPAA-compliant portal. This might expand your options since the commute isn't a factor. Be sure to verify that a therapist is licensed to see clients in your state.

Licensing

It's important to have confidence that your therapist is trained and being held to a board-regulated code of ethics. This protects you and holds them accountable. Look for someone with credentials that indicate they've completed at least a master's degree, have passed a licensing test, and have done numerous internship hours such as Licensed Professional Counselor (LPC), Licensed Marriage and Family Therapist (LMFT), Licensed Mental Health Counselors (LMHC), PsyD, or Ph.D. Someone with "associate" added to the end of their credentials has finished their degree and is working under a clinical supervisor.

Note: Coaches and therapists are not the same thing. Coaches aren't subject to the same code of ethics as therapists. Coaching is appropriate for reaching short-term goals, while therapy is more appropriate for addressing mental illness or processing trauma.

Cost + Insurance

Therapy is not always covered by insurance and most therapists don't accept insurance anymore due to the extremely low reimbursement rates that most insurance companies offer. If you want to try using insurance, make sure your plan covers outpatient mental health treatment (many do not). Otherwise, you'll need to pay "out of pocket". The average therapy session cost is about $150, but if you can't afford that, look for someone who offers a "sliding scale fee". This means they'll lower their fee to work with your budget.

Inquiring

Many therapists get multiple therapy inquiries a day and have limited spots to fill. Plan to reach out to several therapists who meet your criteria instead of banking on one. Include the information below in your inquiry email or voicemail:

- The issue(s) you want to address in therapy (don't be shy!)

- Why you think this therapist will be a good fit for you

- How you plan to pay (insurance or private pay)

- Your preference of in-person or virtual sessions, and

- The general days/times you'd be able to meet.

If the therapist responds that they have an opening, be sure to ask any follow-up questions you have that might save you some time and effort. If they're fully booked, you can ask if they have a waiting list or can recommend someone else.

Paperwork

When you schedule your first session, your therapist will give you paperwork to fill out. You don't need to write a book but be as honest and detailed with your answers as you're comfortable with. Make sure to turn it in early enough so they can read it before you meet with them.

Confidentiality

Licensed therapists are bound by HIPAA privacy laws and are obligated to keep your identity and information confidential. The only exceptions to confidentiality are when someone's safety is at risk or when a court order is involved. If you have any concerns about privacy, ask your therapist.

Expectations

Realistic expectations will set you up for success. A good therapist isn't going to tell you what to do or just sit there nodding. Think of your therapist as a guide who will ask questions and work with you to find solutions. They may challenge your thinking patterns or ask you to talk about difficult topics, but you will still be in charge of making a change.

Remember therapists are people too and they have their own boundaries. If you want to reach out to them in between sessions, make sure you know what their policy is.

Chemistry

Your connection with your therapist matters. Don't let yourself feel stuck with a therapist that you don't trust or don't like just because you've seen them a few times. If you're not comfortable for any reason, it's completely fine for you to leave and find someone else. Your therapist will not take it personally.

Additional Resources

Links to Inventories

www.empathyparadigmtherapy.com/resources

Recommended Media

www.empathyparadigmtherapy.com/media

Finding a Therapist

www.empathyparadigmtherapy.com/tips

Therapist Consultations & Training

www.empathyparadigmtherapy.com/training

Sources

Azim, et al. (2021) Epistles of Dyspareunia: Storying Christian Women's Experiences of Painful Sex. Culture, Health & Sexuality vol. 23,5 (2021): 644-658.

Abrams, et al. (2013) Attachment Theory: Encyclopedia of Behavioral Medicine. pp. 149–155.

Abrams, Z. (2021) Improved Treatment for Developmental Trauma. Monitor on Psychology vol. 52 No. 5.

American Psychiatric Association. (2022) Diagnostic and Statistical Manual of Mental Disorders. 5th ed., Text Revision, American Psychiatric Publishing.

Argyle & Beit-Hallahmi. (2013) The Social Psychology of Religion. Psychology Revivals, Routledge.

Blosnich, et al. (2020) Sexual Orientation Change Efforts, Adverse Childhood Experiences, and Suicide Ideation and Attempt Among Sexual Minority Adults. American Journal of Public Health, vol. 110,7 e1-e7.

Bowlby, Frey, & Ainsworth. (1953) Child Care and the Growth of Love. Penguin Books.

Brown, B. (2012) Daring Greatly: How the Courage to Be Vulnerable Transforms the Way We Live, Love, Parent, and Lead. New York, NY, Gotham Books.

Carlson & Putnam. (1993) An Update on the Dissociative Experiences Scale.

Chaves & Garland. (2009) The Prevalence of Clergy Sexual Advances Towards Adults in Their Congregations.

Cherniak, et al. (2021) Attachment Theory and Religion. Current Opinion in Psychology, Vol. 40 (2021): 126-130.

Denney, et al. (2018) Child Sexual Abuse in Protestant Christian Congregations: A Descriptive Analysis of Offense and Offender Characteristics. Religions, vol. 9, no. 1, Jan. 2018, p. 27.

Domestic Abuse Intervention Project (1993) The Duluth Model: The Power and Control Wheel.

Guidepost Solutions (2022) Independent Investigation Report: The Southern Baptist Convention Executive Committee's Response to Sexual Abuse Allegations and an Audit of the Procedures and Actions of the Credentials Committee.

Herman, J. (2015) Trauma and Recovery. Basic Books.

Human Rights Campaign: Roundup of Anti-LGBTQ+ Legislation Advancing In States Across the Country

Isely & Isely. (1990) The Sexual Abuse of Male Children by Church Personnel: Intervention and Prevention.

Johnson & VanVonderen. (2005) The Subtle Power of Spiritual Abuse. Bethany House.

Jun, et al. (2018). White Jesus: The Architecture of Racism in Religion and Education.

Keller, K. (2016) Development of a Spiritual Abuse Questionnaire.

Kübler-Ross, E. (1969) On Death and Dying. Routledge.

Lifton, R. (1961) Thought Reform and the Psychology of Totalism: A Study of "Brainwashing" in China.

Piaget, J. (1971) The Theory of Stages in Cognitive Development.

Pooler & Barros-Lane, (2022) A National Study of Adult Women Sexually Abused by Clergy: Insights for Social Workers. Social Work, Vol 67.

Raine & Kent, (2019) The Grooming of Children for Sexual Abuse in Religious Settings: Unique Characteristics and Select Case Studies, Aggression and Violent Behavior, Vol 48.

Rotter, J. (1954) General Principles for a Social Learning Framework of Personality Study. Social Learning and Clinical Psychology. Prentice-Hall, Inc

Seligman & Maier. (1967) Failure to Escape Traumatic Shock. Journal of Experimental Psychology 74.1 (1967): 1.

The Religious Trauma Institute. (2019) Adverse Religious Experiences.

The Trevor Project (2023) Ending Conversion Therapy.

Van der Kolk, B. (2014) The Body Keeps the Score: Brain, Mind, and Body in the Healing of Trauma. New York.

Van Deusen & Courtois. (2015) Spirituality, Religion, and Complex Developmental Trauma. Spiritually Oriented Psychotherapy for Trauma, pp. 29–54.

Vaughan, F. (1991) Spiritual Issues in Psychotherapy. Journal of Transpersonal Psychology.

Vieten & Lukoff. (2021) Spiritual and Religious Competencies in Psychology. The American Psychologist.

Walker, L. (2017) The Battered Woman Syndrome. Fourth ed. Springer Publishing Company.

Ward, D. (2011) The Lived Experience of Spiritual Abuse. Mental Health Religion & Culture, pp. 899–915.

Wellwood, J. (1984) Toward a Psychology of Awakening.

Winell, M. (2011) Religious Trauma Syndrome (Series of 3 articles), Cognitive Behavioural Therapy Today; British Association of Behavioural and Cognitive Therapies, London.

Printed in Great Britain
by Amazon

45497025R10126